To Karen & Jessica,
Best Wishes for
a great time of life!
Margo
4/29/04

D1124966

This is a unique and fresh approach to dealing with very real college anxieties and family communication issues. The differing perspectives of student and parent are eye-opening and informative. A great book for families to read together throughout the college years.

Thomas E. McManus
Director of College Counseling,Tatnall School

This excellent guide provides information where little currently exists. The authors' experience and personal candor illustrate how conflict inherent in the separation process can lead both parent and young adult into a mature and balanced relationship.

Sue Crichton, MSS, LCSW

A great resource to use throughout the entire college journey— from acceptance to graduation.

Suzanne Ketcham
Assistant Director of Admission, University of Miami

In my twenty-two years as an educator, rarely have I seen such a unique book. The authors paint a candid portrait of American family dynamics as the children leave the nest for the college experience. Their style is absorbing, their format clever, and the text informative and real. Parents and students will see themselves in this book and realize that they are not alone. I'm sure this book will open many doors to communication between parents and their college-bound children.

Beverly Stewart Cox, M.Ed.
President, Back to Basics Learning Dynamics, Inc.

Once started, it was hard to put down! We have taken the journey through the "doors" twice with our two sons and now are taking it with our daughter. *Doors Open From Both Sides* hits home! It is an excellent guide and we truly wish we had read it when our first born was entering his senior year in high school. We recommend it to all parents and students who are getting ready for their own journey.

Donna and Clark Collins

Doors Open provides practical advice to parents and children on how to understand each other during one of the toughest transition periods of our interdependent lives. With two sons and two daughters between the ages of nine and fifteen, it has, thankfully, opened my eyes for the journey ahead. It will be a good preparation for our family as the children take their first steps away from home. The authors reached both our hearts and heads with their insightful dialogue!

Fred Honold

Doors Open From Both Sides was like a trip down Memory Lane. It touched so many chords in me as I remembered the emotional times. This book also opened my eyes as to what my parents must have been experiencing. For students, it is a must!

Stephanie Tipton
Graduate, University of Miami

Doors
Open
From Both Sides

THE OFF-TO-COLLEGE GUIDE
FROM TWO POINTS OF VIEW:
PARENTS AND STUDENTS

Margo E. Bane Woodacre, MSW
& Steffany Bane

American Literary Press, Inc.
Five Star Special Edition
Baltimore, Maryland

Doors Open From Both Sides

Library of Congress
Cataloging in Publication Data
ISBN 1-56167-680-2

Library of Congress Card Catalog Number:
2001117630

Cover concept & design by Steffany Bane
Chapter illustrations by Margo E. Bane Woodacre
Cover photograph of authors by Dick duBroff, Final Focus
For Better or Worse comics used with permission.

Published by

American Literary Press, Inc.
Five Star Special Edition
8019 Belair Road, Suite 10
Baltimore, Maryland 21236

Manufactured in the United States of America

Dedicated to Angie with love

ACKNOWLEDGMENTS

Many people helped make this book a reality for us. For their support and encouragement over the past four years, we are truly grateful.

Special thanks go to:

- Ernie for his continuous support, insight, and creative editing talents;
- Peter N. Williams and Carolyn Smith for their editing abilities;
- Penny, Kathi, and Sue for their advice and affirmations;
- Mom, Tom, and Bill for their enthusiasm;
- Our friends for their moral support: Evelyn, Vicki, Tami, Ollie, Jill, Stephanie, Patty, Fred, and Irma's Group;
- Our "experts" for their support and good advice: Julianna, Rebecca, Wayne, and Andy;
- Many parents and students for their willingness to share openly their feelings and personal stories;
- Our editor, Alan C. Reese for his patience, advice, and expertise;
- Long mother-daughter walks on school breaks;
- The yellow door on Andover Road.

CONTENTS

When one door closes, another opens, but we often look so long and so regretfully upon the closed door that we do not see the one that has opened for us.
—Alexander Graham Bell

For most of us, going through life's transitions is like opening new doors. As we open them we can discover surprises, new findings, new challenges and new fears. Sometimes, we need to close the doors to put closure on matters. Sometimes, we need to work to keep them open.

One major life transition occurs at the stage when the young-adult child leaves home to go off to college. This transition brings new experiences and challenges for both the parent and the child. Despite having lived under the same roof for a number of years, parents and children inevitably have different perspectives on many aspects of life. Consequently, experiencing the "college separation" can affect them in different ways. This book, written by a mother and her daughter, describes how each saw, felt, and learned from this particular transition. Their two points of view represent both sides of the transition; hence, the title, **Doors Open from Both Sides**.

With the transition come phases that have their own joys, their own challenges and their own fears. The book focuses a chapter on each of these phases and represents them as types of "doors." Drawing on their experiences, the co-authors end each chapter with helpful tips to avoid some of the common traps one can fall into during each phase of the transition.

This book presents specific views of parent and child during what family therapists Carter and McGoldrick (1989) call the "Launching Children and Moving On" stage of life. For the young adult leaving the nest, this stage can be a time of excitement, confusion and fear. It is also the time for him or her to start to differentiate the emotional program of the family, to begin to formulate personal life goals, and, in essence, to start to become an independent self.

For parents of the college-bound child, the process of letting go is not new. In a broad sense, parents start to experience the separation process through events such as their child's stages of toddlerhood, their first days of school, and their first vacation away from home and family. Despite these early experiences, the sense of loss and separation anxiety can be more pronounced when the young-adult child moves off on his or her own, whether to college, to the job away from home, to marry, or to join the service. For the parents left in the empty nest, it is the time to learn to really let go, to redefine personal identity and relationships, and to look ahead to the future.

When young ones leave home, parents realize that they have more personal freedom, but of course, so do their children. In reality, from here on, parents will always have less control over the departing child. The departing young adult feels a growing and sometimes exhilarating sense of freedom. While perhaps not always recognizing it, they still have an ongoing need for continued support and guidance. Often, the needs and views of the two generations and the temperamental relationship of parent and child can become a challenging one. Fortunately, with a mutual commitment to understanding each other, this time of life, despite its stresses, can be rewarding and fulfilling. As Erma Bombeck once wrote in her column:

Wouldn't it be wonderful if parents could look at their teenagers and say, "I want you to stay, but you can't." Wouldn't it be wonderful if teen-agers could look at their parents and say, "I don't want to leave, but I must." It's so much better to close the door gently on childhood than to slam it.

For young adults raised with the security of a home and family for 17-20 years, the transition into independence and freedom is a new experience. For parents who devoted the same amount of time to guiding and supporting their children, this change can create a large, empty hole in their everyday lives. There are no formal guidelines for managing emotions during this important transition. Hopefully, what the writers have learned from writing this book can help its readers in learning how to "gently close the door on childhood."

From the co-authors:

Doors Open from Both Sides was written with love, sweat, and tears. Together, as mother and daughter, we recalled our specific challenges and assessed how they opened our eyes to our differences and our similarities. We drew from the personal journals that we have kept over several years and exchanged ideas through telephone contact, e-mails and visits. Through this communication, we discovered that while we were both going through the same transition, we faced different types of challenges in dealing with it. Together, we decided to write about our experiences.

EMOTIONAL BEGINNINGS
Thoughts from Mom:

September (Journal entry)
My 47 years of life have brought challenges but none has touched my emotions more than the approaching "empty-nest syndrome." This stage has been filled with a mixture of joy, excitement, fears and loneliness. I have become more introspective and questioning about who I am and who I am becoming. Suddenly, I am looking for more meaning to my life. Is this middle age or true growth?

As the mother of an only child (and a single mother for ten years), I worked outside the home but considered motherhood my main job and my joy. To me, the empty-nest syndrome was simply a term to describe the phase of life when parents learn to adjust after their children move out. It sounded so simple! For some parents, it meant the freedom of having their personal lives back. Despite this, I rarely found a parent who didn't feel a sense of uneasiness when approaching this new phase.

Whether the parent faces the departure of an only child, a first, or a last child, the realization begins to set in that life is about to take on a new dimension.

Thoughts from Steff:

Leaving home for the first time can be a scary experience. For me, it was both scary and exciting. During most of my senior year of high school, I *thought* I was ready to go. When accepted into my first-choice college, I *knew* it was the time to go! Doubts soon set in, however, when I thought of all the things I was leaving behind: my familiar day-to-day schedule, special people, personal possessions, and the safety of my bedroom. Most of all, I was leaving my secure life at home. Although these mixed emotions were confusing and bothersome to me, I sensed that the time was right to move on and become more independent.

In high school we talked a lot about "getting out" in the same way prisoners would talk about escaping from jail. We were ready to go off to college, start a job, meet new people, move out of the house and be on our own. When the time actually arrived, however, fears surfaced from out of nowhere!

My choice was to go relatively far away to college. I wanted a college that specialized in my academic interests but also wanted to have my freedom and to prove to others that I could make it on my own. Yes, there were fears and doubts, but I felt it had to be done. I think that Mom wanted to have me closer to home, but she didn't want to stand in my way. At that time, it was important for me to know that I had loving family and friends that supported my decision to move so far from home. With this support, I decided to follow my instincts and my heart. Now, as I look back, I am truly glad I did it.

Chapter 1

THE HIGH SCHOOL SENIOR YEAR
The Revolving Door

Chapter 1..................

THE HIGH SCHOOL SENIOR YEAR
The Revolving Door

Entering the high school senior year is like moving through a revolving door: attention needs to be focused on making a good exit! The senior year calls for careful planning for that exit—whether it be to college or to a job. It is a year of activities that focuses on the child's future. If the goal is college, much of the school year revolves around choosing and getting into a college.

It is also a year for those parents facing an imminent empty nest to reflect upon the past and think about *their* future. Just as high school seniors remind themselves, "this is the last game, the last test, the last dance, the last play," the parents begin to realize that they, too, will be involved in a series of "lasts." Questions suddenly enter one's mind, "What's next?" "How can I handle this?"

Mom

The term, "empty nest" really hit home for me during my daughter's high school senior year:

September (Journal entry)

Today is the first day of Steffany's senior year in high school! Hard to believe, but true. I woke up early thinking about it. I recalled taking her to her first day of kindergarten and shortly thereafter watching her walk independently into the first grade. On both of those occasions, I went home, cried, and asked myself, "Where has the time gone?"

Now years later, I feel like crying again. The next "first" for Steff will be a move toward being out on her own. As a mother, I am aware that an important part of my own life is in major transition, and this change is somewhat frightening. I feel a sense of excitement mixed with a degree of apprehension.

Steff has started her college essays and applications and feels she has a good chance of getting into some of her choice colleges. I am enjoying helping her with these important decisions. It's a busy time in her life and I believe she is ready for the change. I only hope I am!

The first "college night" at the high school was overwhelming to us when we learned about the decisions to be made concerning final SAT schedules, applications, essays, and college interviews. As a somewhat congenital worrier, I felt the pressure to get these chores accomplished. I became torn between my good intention to hand over responsibility to my child and my worry-based impatience to jump in and help her get it done!

Fortunately, Steffany (with some coaxing) was somewhat diligent about meeting her responsibilities and deadlines. Other people became involved with this seemingly large chore. Steff's high school counselor was very important in keeping her on her toes with the deadlines. Her dad helped her with applications and took her on some of the college visits. My husband, her stepfather, supported Steffany by helping proofread her college essays.

Once the college applications were sent in, Steff and I began the anxious wait for responses. For some, acceptances arrived early. The word would come, "So-and-so got accepted." These announcements seemed to place more pressure on us. Steffany had applied for early acceptance; she knew with certainty which college she wanted and had applied to second choices only at the suggestion of her counselor. Steffany's approach had its good points but also had its risks. In her mind, there was only one college for her, and if she were accepted there, her enthusiasm for college would be sky-high. My unspoken fear was that her first-choice college might not select her.

The anticipation for mail delivery matched that of waiting for a lucky lotto number! We had been told that acceptances would be in bulkier envelopes. One day, a thin envelope arrived from her chosen college. I happened to be traveling and felt an intuition to call home. I then listened to a tearful, depressed daughter who felt that her world had ended! Steffany had been deferred. She, at the moment, could not distinguish between *deferred* and *rejected*. She clearly needed a shoulder to cry on. At a thousand miles from home, how helpless I felt!

The universe smiled on Steffany, however, when, during the following month, our mail included a bulky envelope from college choice Number One. I remember pulling it from the mailbox and feeling my heart race. I nervously held it up to the light and attempted to read through the envelope. I did see the word, "Congratulations!" and as a parent, I felt relieved and ecstatic. We had hit *our* lottery!

Throughout the senior year, it had been helpful to share feelings with other parents. At sporting and school events, we would find ourselves talking about joys, fears and the growing sense of sadness about the approaching transition. It was helpful for me to know that I was not alone with my feelings.

I remember one mother telling me:

Each time I drive down the driveway at school, I am aware that I won't be doing this next year and I have a sick feeling in the pit of my stomach. I already have planned an alternate driving route for the next year so I won't have to go by the school!

I also remember Prom Night when many of the parents gathered at each others' homes to take the last high school dance photos. As our well-coiffed, elegant and handsomely dressed young people smiled for the cameras, we shook our heads in disbelief that this was yet another school *last*. We reminisced about the memories of our children's very first dance at middle school and once again asked each other, "Where did the time go?"

Senior year was filled with many emotions and culminated with graduation. For many parents and their children, graduation was an emotional experience. For months, we were wrapped up in the excitement leading up to the actual event and suddenly, there we were, sitting at our final high school event!

The emotions touched fathers and mothers alike. One teary-eyed father of an only child whispered to me as we watched our children receive their diplomas:

It seems like I have been sitting in this gym for five years cheering on Jim's teams. I'm excited for him, but I know I've become very attached to this era, and it saddens me that it's over.

For him and the rest of us, that era *was* over. Now came the college era with its own mixture of feelings.

Steff

Finally a senior! The biggest kids in the school. Ever since I was a preteen, I dreamed of being a senior and "ruling" the school. When senior year arrived, I was ready. This meant senior privileges, my own parking spot, more free time and, not to forget, college was right around the corner! We all threw around the word "college" like it was no big deal, and it felt extremely cool saying it.

I found my long-term friends increasingly important to me as we went along with the flow of our last school year. We had had so many good times, and we cherished them. Now we sensed that our closeness could be ending.

College was becoming more of a reality than an image, however, because of the work on applications, forms and essays that had to be done. Although I had visited my favorite college choices, my mother and I were still making weekend trips to nearby colleges. During this period, my schedule was jam-packed with priorities involving school work, sports and applications. I felt I had never been faced with so many deadlines in my life.

The whole idea of going off to college was exciting: new places, new faces, choice of major and a class schedule that I could select on my own, so much freedom! My friends and I would meet during our breaks at school and chat about how we were ready to graduate. By mid-year, our familiar, robot-like schedules were becoming a bit boring but we still felt comfortable and safe.

Over the past twelve years, I had grown up with the same people at the same school. While summer might find us separating and doing our own things, we would return in the fall to our friends with new stories and experiences to share. I now sensed that the life I was used to was about to change.

Kids react in different ways to their last year in high

school. Some feel few emotional ties to their schools and are ecstatic at the prospect of leaving. However, along with most of my friends, I was starting to feel a bit melancholy about the approaching "end."

Perhaps I felt this first through my involvement in sports. While suiting up for my last basketball game, I suddenly realized that I would never again put on my high school jersey for a game. There were five seniors on our team, and we were all close. After our last game, there was complete silence on our bus ride home. This was when I lost it! My sports career as a senior was now over. My teammates felt it, too. There were so many "what ifs?" clouding my head: What if I don't find happiness out there? What if I don't get the opportunity to play team sports again? What if my friends move on and forget me? This was the first time I truly realized how important this phase of my life had been to me. I began to think about all my *lasts*—my last game, my last prom, my last performance, my last test, my last class—all the way up to my last day as a senior.

At the same time, my focus was on what was ahead. Constantly hanging over my shoulder was the fear of *not* getting accepted into my first choice or any of my college choices. Each day my heart pounded as I checked the mail. Knowing how eager Mom could be, I had asked her not to open any responses from colleges. One day, I returned home to find a thin envelope embossed with my favorite college logo. I tore into it with shaking hands and read, ". . .it is very difficult to get in through early application and your application will be placed in the regular admission." I was devastated! Mom was away and not around to console me. She was the one I needed the most.

Hearing Mom's voice on the phone that night, I got emotional and sobbed like a baby. To me, my fear of not getting accepted had become a reality. Despite my parents assuring me that my chances were still good, I was deeply disappointed, somewhat embarrassed and fell into a slump for the next week. I did not mention the letter to my friends.

As things turned out, I hadn't been rejected. Within the next few weeks, I arrived home to find a thicker envelope from my favorite college. I opened the letter to find a congratulatory letter of acceptance! Mom placed a baseball cap with the college logo on my head (somehow she knew what was in the letter) and I felt on top of the world!

After our celebration, my efforts turned to getting ready for the next phase. Now, I couldn't wait to head off to college. With my biggest fear removed, the road ahead seemed clear and I felt ready for the challenge.

Trap Doors
Tips from Mom for parents:

· **Validate your feelings.**

Accept and respect your feelings during this stage of your life. Facing change is one of the biggest human fears. The *Launching of Children* phase is a major life transition and feelings of apprehension on the part of all family members are normal. Feel thankful to know that these feelings represent a positive attachment between parents and child.

· **Talk about your feelings.**

Share your experience with and get support from your partner, your family or a friend who has been through or is going through this kind of a transition. You will not feel so alone with your feelings, and you might be able to help each other get through this experience.

· **Keep a personal journal.**

A journal can help you express your thoughts and emotions in a very personal and non-threatening form. It will help to acknowledge and validate your feelings. Down the road, it will provide memories of an important period in the life of your child and yourself.

· **For organization, keep lists of "things to do."**

The high school senior year is busy with activities and important deadlines. Keeping a calendar of events and lists of "things to do" and due dates helps everybody move effectively through a hectic schedule.

· **Enjoy the moment.**

There will be exciting and memorable moments during your child's senior year. Make the most of them. Try not to get overwhelmed with the "to do" lists, and take one day at a time.

· **Get help from the college counselor at the high school.**

It is helpful for both the parents and students to get acquainted with the counselor. College counselors know the ropes with the college application system, and they can be a helpful guide along the way.

Tips from Steffany for students:

· **When feasible, visit the campuses of the colleges being considered.**

Certainly try to visit and tour the campuses of your primary choices. It is important to "get a feel" for the environment. If you know someone who is already attending one of your favorite colleges, arrange for a weekend visit. This way, you will capture the true flavor of campus life and have a chance to ask important questions of the current students.

· **Know the difference between "deferred" and "rejected."**

Understand that being deferred is *not* being rejected. Deferrals simply put you on the next list to be considered. (How calmly I can say that now!)

· Don't give up on your goal.

If you receive a deferral or a rejection to your favorite college, don't give up. Write or call the college admissions person or department and, without being critical or defensive, share your disappointment as well as your continuing determination to get in. Colleges *do* want students who really want to be there.

· Be aware that your parents might get on your nerves.

Senior year is so busy with finishing up high school and college applications. Don't be surprised if your parents get on your nerves with constant reminders about things that need to be done. In my case, although Mom was a bit of a pain, she did keep me from procrastinating.

· Don't "wish" your time away!

During your senior year, spend as much time as you can doing something you love to do. . . and spend it with people with whom you want to be. The last year of high school moves so quickly, try to enjoy each moment.

Chapter 2

THE SUMMER BEFORE COLLEGE
The Busy Door

Chapter 2................

THE SUMMER BEFORE COLLEGE
The Busy Door

Families preparing to send a child off to college will
find summer to be unusually busy. Much activity will
be focused on shopping, packing, and preparing for
the move to college. Mail will arrive frequently from the
colleges with information, course selections, applications
for dorms, and schedules for fall classes. Summer will seem
like a whirlwind of activity culminating with an emotional
send-off.

Mom

During these months, I found that my earlier feelings of
apprehension had diminished. The course ahead was set.
My daughter was getting ready for an important step in her
life, and we were working together to get ready for it. At

the same time, I knew that every moment that she spent with family and friends was precious. The friends going on to college shared their own news about potential roommates, school schedules and their general excitement about the new stage in their lives.

Most of my focus was on the necessary shopping, paper work and packing. I followed the lists sent to us from the college, the local "back to school" sales and compared notes with other parents, hoping not to miss anything important with the off-to-college preparation. I tried to include my daughter as much as possible, but she was too busy with her part-time job and social life. I didn't like the fact that *I* was the only one doing the preparation.

By the middle of August, I felt I had accomplished my part in what needed to be done toward Steffany's departure. Suddenly, activity seemed to cease in my role as "transition manager." I became increasingly conscious of the fact that my child was soon to leave the home-nest and venture out into the adult world. It was then that my emotions began to intensify:

August 16 (Journal entry)

Here I sit, looking at clean and pressed clothes folded ready for Steff to pack for college. Her trunk is already filled and closed. Just two days left before the move to Florida. I hear that it is harder before our children leave than it is when they are actually away. I don't know about that. I do know how quiet and lonely this house will be. Oh dear, I'll miss her. I ask myself at this point, "How did my mom deal with my leaving for college so well? I don't remember seeing her anxious or sad, and we were close, too. Why is it so hard for me?"

THE TIME FINALLY ARRIVES

Southern colleges tend to start earlier. For that reason, Steff was one of the first of her friends to leave. How active the night before she left for college! The phone rang nonstop and many of her high school friends came to say good-bye and wish her well. There was laughter and there were tears. Her boyfriend and closest friends stayed until late, waiting as long as they possibly could before having to say "good-bye." I felt it important to give them their privacy. Exhausted from the preparation and surge of activity, I retired early knowing the morning would come all too soon. It did.

First to get up, I found the house quiet. There wasn't much to do. The car was packed. Preparation was over; the move was upon us. I had a long drive ahead. My feelings of fear and sadness began to emerge again:

August 19 (Journal entry)

I woke up early this morning with a gnawing in my stomach. Today is the day that I have thought about over this entire year. . . Steff leaves for college, for real. Life here at home will be so different. I'm already feeling a sense of loss. I have felt this feeling before; it is similar to the feeling I had when my father passed away. Is this normal to feel this way? I don't like the feeling.

ON OUR WAY

The "good-byes" were tearful for my daughter and her best friend. They seemed to hang on to every second together as I went over my checklist for the journey. Finally, the moment came to leave, and we pulled out of the driveway. We were on our way.

Once we got a few miles behind us, our focus began to change. It was as if a fog had been lifted. The emptiness we had felt saying "good-byes" was replaced with the anticipation of new "hellos." Suddenly we could focus on the next step—the actual move into college. On the Auto Train to Florida, we had many uninterrupted hours to spend together and talk about what lay ahead. Steffany even had the chance to meet other young people heading south to various colleges. As we got closer to our final destination, our spirits began to brighten.

Steffany's father joined us at the university in Florida and the three of us shopped for appliances and last-minute necessities. We included everything on the college list until our car could carry no more. As the three of us drove on to the university grounds, we joked that we looked like the Beverly Hillbillies arriving in Hollywood!

On campus, the energy was high. So much to do! Like ants on a mission, students and parents hustled around pushing dollies loaded with luggage, boxes and small appliances. The halls seemed filled with feelings of excitement, nervousness, hope and anticipation.

Steff liked her roommate and made friends very quickly. I dreaded saying good-bye but felt joy for her obvious excitement and good spirits. I was flying home and leaving the car in Florida with her dad. Our farewells were quick; I was off to catch a flight, and she was off to catch a bite to eat with her new-found friends. On my flight home, I remember gazing out the window of the plane and feeling a sense of relief as I recalled my daughter's smiling face running off with five other freshmen to the dining hall. That vision carried me all the way home. As brave as I felt then, little did I know that the hardest part was yet to come.

The summer before I left for school was so busy it seemed like a blur. I worked a part-time job but spent much time with my mother running all kinds of errands to prepare for college. Mom often got on my nerves with all of her prodding and scheduling. I had absolutely no idea of the time, effort and money that could go into preparing for college. At times, I would realize how far away I was going and how my new life was not going to provide the usual comfort of home, familiar school, family and friends. It was a new beginning and what seemed so distant and exciting during my senior year was now more imminent and somewhat frightening.

All of a sudden departure day was upon us. For the first time during the busy summer, I stopped, took a breath, and wondered where all the time had gone. All year I had anxiously awaited this day! Now that it was upon me, I was unsure of how ready I was to face it. It's a lot different talking about something than actually *doing* it.

On Our Way

Saying good-bye to my boyfriend and best friend were difficult for me. The morning I left, I didn't know what to think or how to feel. I felt scared, excited, happy and sad. I wasn't sure if what I was doing was right. Mom and I drove away from my home waving to my best friend who was tearfully sitting on my front step and my stepfather who stood beside her. All of us had our own feelings to deal with. I felt numb. I couldn't look back at my house or my girlfriend. I remember burying my head in the pillow that rested on my lap, and uncontrollably crying. This was a different cry because it wasn't the usual "I need comforting" cry. It was an "I'm confused, What do I do? What am I feeling?" cry. And that made me cry even more.

The Arrival on Campus

The arrival on campus brought butterflies to my stomach. As we entered the campus, I felt as "one" with the car. My face was literally pushed against the glass window because of the full load. . . suitcases, boxes, clothing, appliances and pillows!

It was my choice to move on campus as soon as the schedule permitted. I wanted to get the feel of my room, my dorm and the area. Moving in was a long, exhausting process. There were many trips to the car on a hot August day. Decisions had to be made on the location of personal items, furniture, carpeting and wall hangings. Mom and I unpacked boxes and bags while Dad set up the appliances. It was a tedious process, and I had forgotten how much stuff I had brought.

By mid-afternoon, I was settled into my college home. I had met new faces in my hall but had not yet met my roommate. My fear was that she wouldn't show and I'd be alone. She finally arrived. Although we seemed to have different personalities, we felt a need to stick together and we got along fine. I knew my way around at this point and took her under my wing to help her accomplish the procedural part of checking in. This felt good.

The departure of my parents was near. It was difficult saying good-bye to them as I tried not to appear upset. . . just a thank you and a quick unemotional hug. I was worried about Mom crying since I knew that would start me crying. A group of new friends waited for me to join them to the dining hall, so off I went. The truth was, I wanted to run after my parents and yell, "Okay, this was really nice, now let's go home." But I knew this was it. I had to take control of myself and be an adult; after all, I was one.

Trap Doors
Tips from Mom for parents:

· **Expect and accept emotional eruptions both at the time of your child's departure from home and the time you drop your child off at college.**

Be prepared. The departure can be an emotional experience for you as well as your young adult. Tempers can flair or tears can flow. After all, tensions have been building up all summer long for this event.

- **As a parent, go through and read carefully the reams of information sent from the college.**

Keep a file for all of this information and don't depend upon your child to read it alone. You will find helpful tips and important directions on schedules, shopping, packing and move-in that should not be missed.

- **For help in packing, pull from college lists and the advice of others who have gone through the process.**

A shopping list of college necessities for the freshman year is most helpful while preparing for the move. Colleges often send these lists with the orientation materials. If one is not made available, ask a parent who has recently sent a child off to school if she has one to lend you. Don't count on your own instincts to know what is needed. It is amazing how much you may *not* think of!

- **Get a 1-800 phone card for your student to be able to call home.**

A 1-800 number allows your child to call home from any place in the continental U.S. We used this as an "emergency" way for our daughter to call home if she was outside the college campus. Rates are reasonably priced and the card will provide peace of mind all around.

- **Set "house rules" for non-emergency long distance calls *before* the move.**

Many students will want to regularly check-in with their friends from home at their various locations. This practice can result in a very expensive phone bill! E-mail is a much less expensive way to keep in touch. If the student does not own a computer, each school has a computer lab that can provide the use of one.

- **Talk financial responsibilities before the move.**

It is important to communicate openly with your child on money issues. Decide what the respective responsibilities are for parent and child and set limits when necessary.

· **Meet the Resident Assistant (R.A.).**

On move-in day, it is important to meet the resident or hall assistant. Most dormitories will have a meeting during the orientation program to introduce the floor and resident assistant to the parents. If there are any future concerns regarding your child (health, whereabouts, etc.), this is the person, outside of the roommate, who can be contacted. It is not the R.A.'s responsibility to "parent" your college student, but it is their responsibility to keep an eye out for potential dangers or serious problems.

· **Bring the necessary tools.**

Several times during the freshman move-in, we wished we had the essential tools of a hammer, nails, pliers, hooks and screw driver. We had everything else. Take adhesive hooks that can be used on the concrete walls of the dorms and on the backs of doors and in closets. They are great for holding towels, bathrobes, laundry bags, jackets, hats, purses, and many items.

Tips from Steff for students:

· **Saying good-bye to family and friends can be difficult.**

No one could have prepared me for the feelings I had as I left my best friend and my boyfriend behind. I felt frightened and lost. Allow yourself to feel the sadness of the good-byes and know that, with time, everything will feel better.

· **Call your assigned roommate for an introduction and to discuss how you will share getting the necessities for the room.**

The college will send you the name and phone number of your assigned roommate. Make contact with her/him. It might feel uncomfortable at first but it breaks the ice and helps each of you to plan what to bring to the new living quarters.

· Dorm life.

I had the opportunities to live both in single sex and co-ed environments in college. Eventually, I liked both although, at first, I found the coed living arrangements a little less comfortable. Perhaps if I had been raised in a family with brothers, I would have felt differently. The discomfort did not last long, however. After a short while, except for not being able to share clothing and accessories with my male neighbors, everything was the same as in a single-sex dorm. We hung out together, visited each other's rooms and enjoyed college life. Most of the time, the polite habit of "knocking before entering" is practiced.

· Pack light, if at all possible.

I think it is common that students pack three times the clothing they need or will ever use. I was warned of this before I left, and I still managed to bring enough clothing for the whole floor and probably enough shoes for the entire community!

· Leave expensive valuables at home.

Unfortunately, theft can be a reality on campus. Any valuable jewelry, watches or other valued items should not come to school. Do not forget to lock your dorm door when you are not in the room.

· Consider waiting to buy some of the appliances at school.

Many colleges allow appliance dealers and stores to sell small refrigerators, microwave ovens, and carpeting on school property during check-in day and at good prices. Compared with bringing these items, this approach can save a lot of time, space and hassle.

· For those who fly or take the train to college, box and mail some of your items.

· Include pads of stick-on notes in your packing.

I found stick-on notes great for check lists and ideal for leaving reminders to myself and messages to my friends throughout the school year. Placed strategically, they can't be missed.

- **Update your address book and pack stationery and stamps.**

During the summer, I updated my address book with school and e-mail addresses of my closest friends. I took plenty of note cards and a roll of stamps with me to school. It made it easy to write, stamp and pop the letter in the dorm mailbox.

- **Bring quarters for laundry.**

Getting change for the washer and dryer in the dorm can be challenging. Come prepared with some rolls of quarters.

- **Having a car on campus.**

I did not have a car on campus during my first year. I missed having access to one but learned how to get around. Most campuses have transport alternatives to get you where you need to go. However, having my car join me during my sophomore year brought me a new sense of freedom! I could shop, go into the city, and go places on weekends.

There are some drawbacks to having the car: Everyone becomes your friend in order to "bum" a ride (to the stores, parties, sporting events, airport, bus or train station, you name it); Finding parking on campus can be next to impossible since colleges are very strict in policing parking. If you don't have a designated sticker, you *do* get tickets! These tickets can keep you from graduating if they are not paid. And lastly, the costs of the car can be expensive. Gasoline and general upkeep can be costly on a college student's budget.

Chapter 3

THE STUDENT AT SCHOOL, PARENT AT HOME
Doors Apart

Chapter 3..............

THE STUDENT AT SCHOOL, PARENT AT HOME

Doors Apart

The whirlwind of the summer before college is behind us. Two separate doors now exist: the one at home and the one on campus. For parents, the challenge is to adjust to a more stable yet perhaps too quiet homefront. For the young adult, the challenge is to adjust to a more dynamic and unaccustomed habitat. For both the parents and the child, the changes in their environments can produce a variety of emotions.

Mom

HOME QUIET HOME

My own Master's studies in Social Work covered the many stages of the life cycle including the *Launching*

Children stage. At the time of study, I seemed to understand the key principles of this stage enough to write a paper about it. My studies helped me to better understand the empty-nest syndrome in an intellectual sense but did not prepare me personally for what I was about to experience.

Our house now seemed abnormally quiet. The phone didn't ring as much. The familiar sounds of chatter were gone, as were the whispers, the music, and the laughter from my daughter's upstairs room. Any reminders of her that remained—a book bag, sneakers, her key ring, the yearbook—all helped bring a heavy feeling to my stomach and tears to my eyes. I actually changed my traffic pattern around the house so that I would not have to walk by her room.

The reality of this emptiness in my life hit me when I went grocery shopping for the first time after Steffany had left home. Suddenly, I was shopping only for my husband and myself. I felt sad as I walked to the aisle of Steff's favorite cereals and sadder as I passed her favorite snacks. There was now no need to add these to my cart so I passed by quickly, but I couldn't hold back my tears. I felt as empty as my cart looked. I finished shopping as quickly as I could, loaded the car and sobbed all the way home.

Fall, my favorite season, was approaching, but my usual excitement wasn't there. I stayed busy with my work and home projects, but no matter how hard I tried to move on, some emptiness stayed with me morning and night.

September 9 (Journal entry)

I'm tired. I shed some tears as I went in Steff's room tonight and plopped on her bed. It felt so familiar. The room smells of her fragrances and her high school book bag sits on the floor. I thank God for the relationship Steffany and I have, and I tell myself that this is a normal stage to go through.

This is a __big__ transition for me. I believe I'll get through it fine, but it seems so hard right now.

I continued talking to other parents who were experiencing this phase of life and found that I was not alone. One father told me of his experience:

My wife and I planned a two-week vacation after we checked our only son into college. Neither of us could bear the thought of coming home to an empty house.

When we returned, we closed his bedroom door because we couldn't look at his unusually neat and empty room. It remained closed until he returned home for the holidays.

A single mother shared:

I empathize with those who have found themselves in a house echoing with the memories of days gone by. For me, my work filled my daytime hours but I dreaded coming home to the deathly silence of my house.

Steffany's father and I are divorced and although Steffany lived with me and my husband, her father had remained supportive and involved in her life. I wondered if he was feeling the same emptiness that I was. I felt a little relieved and more normal when I found that he, too, missed her and found himself phoning her at school often. Hearing this, I did not feel alone in my loneliness.

AWAY FROM HOME—INDEPENDENCE!

College was nothing like I had ever expected. Adjustment to life without my parents nearby was easier than I thought. At times, however, when I felt alone, I felt a little scared. I knew that all of us freshmen had our own adjustments to make. Some of my new friends described feelings similar to mine. I could often see the same look in their eyes that I had: the "I'm not sure how to feel" look. It was comforting to find that my feelings were quite normal.

I met some wonderful people during the first few days and the students on my floor (twenty-nine girls) seemed to get along well. Together, we would plan floor dinners, decorate our hall for competitions, go out together and celebrate each other's birthdays as well as play pranks on each other. My busy schedule kept my mind occupied and helped me to adjust as the days went by.

ORIENTATION

The Orientation days were great! Interactive games threw us together and proved to be a good way of getting to meet each other. I found that those who went to orientation were glad they did. Some of the people we met ended up being our best friends. Later, we talked about the famous first impressions we had of each other; some were terribly wrong, some were right on. After the Orientation period, the start of classes came as a rude awakening. I think some of us had almost forgotten why we were at school! (You mean, this isn't just one big party?)

Trap Doors

Tips from Mom for parents:

- **Allow yourself to feel the sadness that you may experience in an emptier house.**

The empty nest transition is a big event that can stir up deep emotions for many parents. Letting go of the day-to-day role of parenting is not easy. Many years of one's life have been focused on parenting at home and a newly quiet household can feel unfamiliar and uncomfortable. It is normal to feel sadness and a sense of loss.

- **Volunteer your time.**

If time allows it in your personal life, get involved with a community activity or charity to help fill some of the empty spaces on a calendar once filled by your child's activities.

If you miss the voices of young ones, volunteer at a youth center or club.

- **Grocery shop for your child's favorite items and send care packages.**

Shopping for care packages to periodically send to your child can help cure your empty feeling at the grocery store and cure your child's empty stomach for goodies from home!

- **Resurrect your old dreams.**

It is your turn! Get involved in something that you have wanted to take part in and previously did not have enough time to do. Go back to school, take a class, play a sport, join a health club, or take up a hobby. In her book, *Passages*, Gail Sheehy(1976), suggests:

It is not through caregiving that a woman looks for a replenishment of purpose in the second half of her life. It is through cultivating talents left half finished, permitting ambitions once piggybacked, becoming aggressive in the service of her own convictions rather than a passive-aggressive party to someone else's.

Tips from Steff for students:

- **Pat yourself on the back for early progress you make.**

For some of you, moving away from home might be the hardest adjustment you've yet had to make. You leave the comfort and security of your own home in exchange for what seems like a 2x2 square foot room with a person you have been matched up with by a computer. You are initially unfamiliar with the campus, where classes are, and you are forced to meet people and make new friends. This isn't easy.

- **Don't question your actions and decisions too much.**

You have been raised with parental supervision and advice for 17-18 years. Now is the time to learn to test your own instincts about new situations and relationships. You might have a negative "gut" feeling if you are in an uncomfortable situation. Don't ignore it. It is wise to be extra careful the first few weeks of school, as you do not know all the people around you well (although you may think you do). This is not to say don't trust anyone but trust your own judgments first, and, in awkward situations, take charge if no one else will.

· **Be patient with your adjustment to your new environment.**

Once the busy orientation schedule is over, you are faced with the reality of college: academics; new schedules; new living quarters; a new person sharing your quarters (in most cases); and new pressures along with new freedom. At times, you may feel out of your comfort zone. This is completely normal. Be patient, it takes time to adjust.

· **Take part in the Orientation Program.**

I recommend going through the orientation process. While it may seem silly to some students, you really do meet people. Later, during my sophomore year, I actually chose to work on the orientation staff which was even more fun!

Special tips for the student's first semester:

· **Procrastination and poor study habits.**

It is important not to let yourself form bad study habits in the beginning of school. Many freshmen mess up their first semester because they get so involved in all the peripheral activities around them. It is easy to let academics become secondary. Students might never have had the chance to oversleep for their 8:00 a.m. class in high school but, in college, it is so easy to roll over and hit the "snooze" button. Assignments can fall behind easily, and the consequences can jeopardize your entire semester. It is important to make the effort to stay disciplined through the tough schedule and the unpopular 8:00 a.m. classes. This can help you to develop and ingrain good habits for the semesters to follow.

Much of the motivation behind doing my best in school was wanting to remain right where I was! It wasn't always easy for me to keep up with my assignments but at least I made the effort.

· Gaining weight at school.

Be aware that during the first semester, weight can sneak up on you. Let's talk about the "freshman fifteen." This is the weight that a female swears she will *never* gain (only to come home after four months to find her old high school clothes snug in the hips and pulling at the waist). Could it be the beer? The starchy cafeteria food? Or maybe it's the midnight pizza runs? No matter what the reason, many male and female students tend to put on some weight.

I swore I would *never* gain a pound when I left for school. At first, with the excitement of the move and the freshman activity, I lost weight, but it took no time for me to become relaxed and appreciate how good the soft-serve ice cream, the dry sugary cereals and snacking foods were, and how delicious pizza could taste at 1:00 a.m. All of this led to the reality of weight gain.

I tried several diets, all of which I eventually dropped. It was funny coming home to Mom and telling her my new secrets for weight-loss. She just listened, smiled, and kept quiet. I think she knew it was just a *phase.*

Special tips for the first semester for parents:

· Phases.

"Phase" is a word every parent should get used to since college students can go through many. Phases today include body piercing, tattooing and adopting different styles in clothing and behavior. Parents need to recognize that these changes represent phases and that in almost all cases, the purple hair will not be purple forever. Parents should express their feelings but in a balanced way. Silence can be interpreted as "approval" and heavy criticism can bring on strong resistance. The more understanding and tactful a parent is in discussing the phase, the more likely it is that it will not stick.

· **Try not to put too much pressure on your child regarding specific grade expectations before school starts.**

Encourage the student to try to get off to a good start in the new environment but don't be overly critical if initial grades are not quite up to expectations. It is difficult enough to adjust to the new atmosphere, schedules and college-level classes. Be patient and give your child a little time to settle in before placing any undue pressure on him or her.

Chapter 4

COMMUNICATION WITH SENSITIVITY
The Screen Door

Chapter 4..............

COMMUNICATION WITH SENSITIVITY
The Screen Door

A screen door allows for an open view while at the same time affording a degree of privacy. Similarly, communication between parents and their child away at college should have openness in expressing viewpoints but, at the same time, it should demonstrate a mutual respect for privacy. Staying in touch with each other is important because without communication, there is no connection and worry can take over. All involved should try to be sensitive in listening to, understanding and dealing with special concerns or needs that arise whether they be from the student, parents, siblings or friends.

For the happy student adjusting well at school, calls to home can be infrequent. This is not necessarily a cause for parents to worry. While parents are naturally curious about what their child is up to, the majority of students are busy getting acclimated to their new home, making new friends and adjusting to new schedules and activities. The fact is that without any deliberate malice, they can spend little time thinking about home and they may not appreciate the degree of their parents' normal curiosity.

For the student who is not adjusting well at school, calls to home will probably be made more frequently or, in some cases, rarely or not at all. This circumstance can bring a challenging period for both parent and child. For the parents at home, it can be terribly disturbing to sense their child is unhappy. It is difficult to judge how we should react to this challenge: as protectors, we want to bring our children home to the safety and security of our nest; in our parent-teacher role, we want to cut the cord and allow our child the opportunity to make it on his/her own.

For the student away at school, unhappiness can be lonely and frightening and in some cases, it can lead to depression and illness. There is a sense of embarrassment for some homesick students who fear that Mom or Dad will get upset with their inability to cope with the new environment. This is especially true when the homesick one sees peers adjusting somewhat flawlessly. No matter what the circumstances are that have created unhappiness, communication between parent and child must remain open, honest and in balance.

Mom

STAYING IN TOUCH

I was fortunate to have a child who was happy at school. Indeed, *I* was the one suffering. To my surprise, I didn't hear much from Steffany after she left for school. My thoughts were with her every day. I wondered about her classes, activities, new friends, and her overall adjustment to the university. I wanted to call to check on her often but kept trying to tell myself that it wasn't right to do this too frequently. After all, I didn't want to clip her fledgling wings of independence! At the same time, I was feeling melancholy about her absence and didn't want her to hear the sadness in my voice. When I would call, she was often busy and unable to talk and would tell me she would call me back. I would actually wait by the phone to receive her returned call and, in some instances, wait for a while before realizing that she had probably become distracted.

On these occasions, I would feel disappointed and somewhat rejected. I tried to tell myself I was pleased that she remained busy, but the reality was that I missed our chats and wondered if our bond was beginning to weaken. At times, I felt angry. What happened to her commitment to call me back? I knew I would drop anything for her. Why wouldn't she do the same for me? How important was I in her new life? Sometimes I felt worried. Is she all right? What if she is afraid to tell me otherwise?

I had many reflective moments during the absence of our personal contact. I put myself in *my* mother's shoes when I remembered how I, as a busy young career woman, was always on the run. My mother would call, I would be too busy to talk, promise to return the calls, and sometimes let *her* down. I was now living the moments that my mom would warn me about when she would say, "Wait until you are a mother, you will understand." That understanding had finally come.

Now, Steffany was in my younger, active shoes with a life that was full and less accessible to me. I was waiting at home, with a life that sometimes seemed in limbo or suspended. I began to feel powerless, lonesome, and neglected.

After a lot of internal turmoil with weeks of phone tag and abbreviated chats, I called Steffany and openly shared (in tears) that I missed our "visits" and badly needed one. I suddenly felt like the child crying out for the parent. Steffany, taken back by my emotion, reacted at first with surprise but eventually with empathy and decisiveness.

Together, we set a time for our first, unhurried phone visit since we had been separated. This worked. We both seemed to enjoy our conversation and decided to schedule Sunday afternoons or evenings as our "visiting time." It was not easy for me to admit my feelings to my daughter but I was glad I did it. I tried to openly share my needs with her *without* trying to make her feel guilty.

For the parent of the student who is not adjusting well to his/her new environment there can be different challenges. One mother shared the following about her experience:

Jenny had always been happy and loved high school. Her friends were important and she was busy with many activities. This all changed when she went away to college. She was terribly homesick. She called home 2-3 times a day. Since we were separated by many miles, I could only listen and offer advice over the phone. While my heart was breaking for her, I tried to remain strong and to stay "upbeat" for her as I knew that she was looking to me to evaluate the situation and help her handle it. I tried to tell her to take one day at a time.

It was painful for me not to be able to help more. I would hang up with a sinking feeling. I would cry. The feeling was so helpless. I found it difficult to focus on my job and life at home. I wanted to go to the college, pull her out and bring her home to safety with me!

The experience for parents with a clearly unhappy child can be harrowing particularly if there is a significant geographical separation. It is very difficult to assess the situation from a distance. Lacking a clear understanding of the situation, it is difficult to judge whether to jump in and help or let go and let the child learn to cope.

Most of the time, with proper support, the unhappy

student eventually adjusts. The best advice to the parent is to be patient and try to remain calm. Being available to listen to your child's unhappiness properly validates his or her feelings, but you should avoid taking a proactive position too quickly. If the unhappiness does not go away, setting a time-goal will help make the situation more manageable. For example, suggest to your child to try to make it through Thanksgiving so he or she can reevaluate the situation with the support of family and friends. By Thanksgiving vacation, the student has only a few weeks before Christmas break and the end of the semester. If it is concluded that a change needs to be made, it can be done at the break between semesters.

Without question, there are situations when the school is indeed not the right one for your child. Even when this is the case, trying to make it through at least one semester can provide a good opportunity to assess the situation properly and lay the groundwork for a well-considered change.

COMMUNICATION THROUGH THE INTERNET

Oh, the miracles of technology! Once my daughter was on-line at the university, our communication improved dramatically. E-mail provided a new way for us to "visit" even if schedules did not permit a direct conversation. I was updated on her school studies, activities and social events a couple of times a week. She remained open to sharing her activities with me and most of the time, I was thankful for this. As a certified worrywart, I occasionally would receive an e-mail from her that would have my heart pounding as I read it. Many of these were after Steffany had returned home from social events in the wee hours of the morning. The best consolation for me was that she was home writing them, so I knew she was safe!

One such occasion occurred the morning after Halloween. I remember reading Steff's eyewitness account of an off-campus, community costume party involving an unruly crowd in the mall, a police response with tear gas, and a walk home with three friends at three in the morning. Certainly, if she had shared this with me in person, my facial expressions and my tone of voice would have given away my worry and disapproval. However, through the electronic medium, she felt safe to tell all and was unaware of my mouth hanging open with fear! I was given the chance to calm down before I responded with careful thought.

Communicating through e-mail tends to remove the verbal and nonverbal messages that we can project in person or on the phone. The recipient is not influenced by negative body language or tone of voice. The recipient is also able to read the message more than once to digest and weigh the information before replying. On the other hand, e-mails can never be altered. Words need to be chosen carefully if an important message is being communicated.

E-mail served as a form of journaling, too. When Steffany felt down or overwhelmed with school and personal situations, e-mail offered her a chance to share feelings in writing. I responded through this medium with supportive, upbeat messages or quotes. She told me later that she printed some of these messages and put them on her bulletin board as positive reminders or affirmations.

Even with all the new ways to communicate, let us not forget the time-tested merits of the US Mail! I enjoyed sending cards, letters and packages to Steffany. Often, I would clip out newspaper articles concerning her school, local events and topics of interest and gather them into a large envelope to send at the end of the week. I regularly sent greeting cards and occasionally put together a package of things that I knew she would enjoy.

STAYING IN TOUCH

Initially, Mom seemed to call fairly often and at the busiest of times for me. Sometimes, I couldn't talk to her at that moment and unfortunately, forgot to call her right back. At first, I felt she was trying to make me feel guilty for not keeping in touch. I occasionally wondered if she didn't trust me and was checking up on me.

I didn't think much about the effect my leaving home had on my mom until one day when I received an emotional call from her to tell me that she missed our "visits." I was surprised and, at first, felt somewhat uncomfortable but then realized that she actually missed me, not only as a daughter, but as a friend. This gave me a good feeling but I wasn't sure what to do to soothe her pain. I remember apologizing to her and telling her that I understood her feelings. It was touching for me. I really hadn't noticed that I wasn't calling. I was focusing on my life at school. At Mom's suggestion, we scheduled a convenient time that would allow us more time to talk. I liked the idea, too.

I must admit that I loved my freedom at school to come and go as I pleased. I had no curfews and no parents worrying about my whereabouts. When I occasionally got homesick, my instinct was to stay active. I got involved with rush for a sorority, ran for a student government position, sunk myself into my studies, and worked on meeting new people. It might have been some form of escapism for me, but it worked.

I had my low points, however, even though they were not for extended periods of time. On occasions, I would handle them on my own and not mention the problem to Mom for a week or so. At other times, I would need to pick up the phone and hear my mother's voice. Our relationship was definitely changing. Sometimes I was ready to be independent from her, other times, I was more dependent on her. As I look back, I now understand that this had to be confusing to Mom because the tone of my verbal contacts tended to be erratic.

Communication through the Internet

E-mail is the best thing ever created. This was my connection to the outside world and it was free! Money can wear thin when you're a college student, so e-mail was a perfect way to stay connected. Through electronic mail, I stayed in touch with my friends who were at various colleges all over the country.

I kept in touch with Mom on e-mail, as well. Through this system, I could contact her at *any* hour and fill her in on the happenings of the day or night. I could sit at the computer at 4:00 a.m. and type her a long message without waking her up. With e-mail, it doesn't matter what time you transmit, the receiver gets the message on his or her own schedule!

Oddly, with this form of communication, Mom and I seemed to get closer. I was able to share things with her that I wouldn't have shared face to face, and surprisingly my mother was pretty cool by the time she responded! I looked forward to her e-mails as I did her letters and cards.

For most students, running to the mailbox each day is a norm. The only let down is finding an empty box. Receiving mail always cheered up my day. It didn't matter whether it was a note, a card, a letter or a package, I loved it! My mom and my dad sent things to me on a regular basis. Sometimes I felt sorry for my roommate who received less mail. When I mentioned this to Mom, she included an occasional note to my roommate or sent baked goods in a combined package to *both* of us.

Trap Doors
Tips from Mom for parents:

· **Stay in touch with your child.**
Work out a schedule with your son or daughter for phone calls. The new student's schedule is extremely busy with

the first semester's activities and adjustments. It is important to plan a day and time convenient for both of you.

As time permits, send notes, cards or letters. Few students enjoy checking an empty mailbox! Include clippings from the local papers that might interest them and articles regarding their high school and the home community.

- **Give your child space and don't overdo your phone calls.**

Understand that your child is needing to feel his/her independence. As parents, this is difficult to grasp since we have been at the controls for most of our young one's life. It is time for the child to learn control and responsibility for him/herself. Stay in touch but, absent any warning signs, start to let go and trust.

- **Use the power of e-mail.**

Communicate through e-mail. As mentioned previously, this form of communication is much more open. It is amazing what your student can and will share with you through this medium. We, as parents, can receive the messages, react and have time to reflect before responding.

- **Be aware of "signals" of unusual behavior from your child.**

Look for hints of chronic homesickness or persistent avoidance from your child. If unusual behavior is recognized, look to get help through the proper college channels. This topic is further covered in chapter five on "Emergencies."

Tips from Steff for parents:

- **On keeping in touch:**

Understand all of the things your child has going on. Your student might not call you everyday, for a couple of days or even a week. He or she may have no idea how you are feeling because of the busy school schedule. This is actually a good sign because your child is more than likely adjusting on his/her own. Don't worry! Hopefully, you have instilled in them a sense of morals and good behavior.

Don't question yourself and your child-raising techniques at this stage. All you can do is think positively and pat yourself on the back that your child has made it this far. She will do her best. Also understand your children *will* make some mistakes! Take it easy if they do, as you can do nothing to change what has happened. At these times, be a good listener. Hopefully, if the mistake is not a major one, you can be a listening ear, instead of a lecturing parent.

· **Don't call at 8:00 a.m. (especially on weekends).**

Our hours are now much different from yours. Understand and respect the different schedules when you call.

· **Don't embarrass us!**

Sometimes a parent's worry can lead to overkill with emotional calls and expressions of concerns (sometimes inappropriately shared with the roommate). Unless there is an emergency or chance of danger, try to chill and don't "over-worry."

· **Don't forget the U.S. Mail.**

Send things through the mail! Freshmen love to find the mailbox filled with surprises. This keeps them in touch with home. Packages are really appreciated!

For students:

· **Keep in touch with your parents.**

It is difficult realizing how important it is to our parents that we keep in touch. They may worry too much, that's true, but trust that this is based on love and affection. They have little control over what you do while you're at school, so it won't hurt being five minutes late to a party, to listen to a short lecture from Mom or Dad about making sure you get home safely.

If you actually listen carefully to what your parents say, you'll find that most of the time, their advice isn't half bad. Although it might have been "light years" in the past, the chances are that they have been through situations similar to the ones you're experiencing (hard to believe but true).

· **Except for emergencies, don't call home after midnight.**

Respect your parents' schedules and don't call them at your late hours.

· **Contact with friends from home.**

It is important to maintain your connections with your friends from home but don't overdo it to the point that you are not allowing yourself the chance to meet new friends at college.

Chapter 5

THE CHALLENGES AWAY FROM HOME
Emergency Doors

Chapter 5...............

THE CHALLENGES AWAY FROM HOME
Emergency Doors

Watching their young adults venture out on their own can be a new experience for parents. It may be the first time they have no proximity to their offspring who are facing new kinds of challenges: missing old friends, striving for new relationships in an unfamiliar setting, coping with sickness or even depression while outside the comforting environment of home. For parents who sense their children's challenges from a distance, there can be unaccustomed feelings of helplessness, worry and sometimes frustration and anger.

For students facing challenges away at school, being on their own can be frightening. Young adults need to be able to reach out for help when necessary. It can be difficult for them to learn the healthy balance between dependency and personal responsibility.

Dr. Mom

Mom's homemade chicken soup isn't just a meal;
it is the culinary equivalent of a hug.

At times, my daughter's challenges created in me a large dose of worry which I then carried around until I *knew* that everything was okay. I remember the first call I received from her when she was sick. How powerless I felt! I wanted to be doctor-mom again: to feel her forehead; take her temperature; tuck her in, and fix her my homemade chicken soup. . . and I couldn't. She refused to go to the college infirmary. I could only suggest remedies over the phone. With no influence over the situation, my worries grew: What if she has a serious illness? Her neck is sore, could it be meningitis? Who is going to take care of her? One worry built upon another and I finally called our family doctor to ask for advice. I spent a sleepless night waiting anxiously to hear from Steffany the next day.

When morning finally arrived, I called. My heart was pounding as the phone rang several times with no response. Fear took over. Frantic thoughts raced through my mind: How could I reach her? What if she is too sick to answer her phone? I tried all morning until I finally reached her. I learned that she had visited the infirmary, received the necessary medicine and was feeling better. I realized, at that moment, that the "control" I should be striving for was over my own fears.

Some situations, of course, are more serious and can develop into real emergencies. One mother shared with me the array of emotions she felt when her daughter became ill with mononucleosis:

It was one of the most difficult times of my life as a parent. We enthusiastically sent our daughter off to her freshman year. On a Friday, three weeks into her arrival, I received a call from her: she felt tired, had swollen glands and a painfully sore throat. While I worried about her being ill, her dad felt it was simply a case of homesickness. I wanted to believe that he was right, but my instinct told me that she had something serious. I called our local doctor who recognized that the symptoms were those of mononucleosis and she was told to get immediate bed rest.

I sat helplessly at home. By Monday, she had checked herself into the school infirmary where she was tested and found to have mono. She rested for a couple of days and, worried about falling behind in classes, went back to her heavy workload. Her health seemingly got worse. I couldn't sleep at night worrying about her. Finally, I decided to drive 5 hours to see her.

I was shocked to find my daughter thin and listless. My worry was now joined by guilt for not acting sooner! The decision was immediately made to bring her home where she could get more personal medical attention and rest. I worked out the details with the university's enrollment office that very day while she slept in her room. Bed rest at home was the best prescription and her first semester was delayed.

In this parent's case, getting involved was imperative. Calling the family doctor for guidance helped her and her daughter to assess the possibilities of a more serious illness. With this kind of evidence of a real problem, it is far better to play it safe than to be sorry.

MOM—THE THERAPIST

I remember the concern I felt when I received calls from my child regarding emotional and relationship challenges at school. These were sometimes tearful and could involve her studies, friends, feelings of being overwhelmed by her schedule or even broader questions about her life and where it was taking her. It was often difficult for me to avoid interrupting to offer my own advice. I tried to listen, ask how she felt it should be handled, and then give my advice.

After she had unloaded, *I* would carry this challenge on my mind until we spoke again. Often, when we did speak again, I found a more positive and back-to-normal child who could barely remember the issue and would tell me I worry too much!

It became clear to me that "unloading" her emotions on me was cathartic for her and stressful for me. One childcare expert describes this interaction as the child getting into the "safety zone." The child's instinct is to pass on the worry to one of the parents. Once the worry is shared with the parent, it relieves the child and puts the worry on the parent's shoulders. This occurs at an early stage of development for our children and can continue through adult life within typical parent-child relationships. Parents themselves need to learn to let go of the worry or it becomes a stressful burden for them to carry. This is easier said than done.

MORE SERIOUS EMERGENCIES

Along with illness, other serious challenges can develop while the child is away at school. Depression, alcohol and drug abuse and eating disorders can take over your child's life. The results can be devastating to the child, the parent, and sometimes the entire family. Another mother shared her experience concerning a daughter who had developed a serious eating disorder:

We were frequently in touch with Molly during her first semester away at school. She sounded active and happy. During her visit home for Christmas break, I learned she was suffering from an eating disorder. I had recognized something different about her when she first came home but was not quite sure what it was. She seemed withdrawn and tired and looked thinner in the face but I thought that the stress of her midterms might be the reason. While home, Molly ate out with her friends most of the time but joined us for our family holiday dinner. I remember seeing her push her food unenthusiastically around the plate, but thought little about it.

One morning, I surprised her as I walked into her room with her clean laundry and found her getting dressed. I was shocked at what I saw! Before me, stood a frail skeleton of a once healthy looking body which happened to be that of my own daughter! I sat on her bed and wept. What was she doing this for? Why had I not noticed this until now? Was I a bad mother? What do we do about this? I felt guilt, anger, confusion and empathy all at the same time. My daughter seemed to resent my troubled reactions.

Molly, active with sports in high school, had always kept an eye on her weight. But I had no idea of the obsession she had acquired once she began to put on some pounds during her first semester away. She also had a painful breakup with her high school sweetheart after the first few weeks of school. I did not realize that all of this could have such a traumatic effect on my daughter.

Unfortunately, her father and I did not initially handle things well. We got angry with Molly, reprimanded her and generally treated her like a small child. We told her that we were "pulling" her out of school until she straightened herself out. This created a bigger wedge between us as a family. Finally, through advice from a friend, I contacted a therapist who helped us see things differently.

Though initially against my daughter's wishes, we got professional help as a family. Molly did not return to school in the spring and took a part-time job. It took a year of working together through family therapy before we began to see positive results. It turned out that there were bigger issues that we, as a family, needed to face. As uncomfortable and painful as this experience was, we grew closer as a family. As I look back on that day during Christmas break, I often wonder whether she would still be alive if I had not walked in on her as I did.

Another mother shared her harrowing experience when her daughter became involved with drugs during her first year at college:

When my daughter came home in the spring, she was truly a different person. She was no longer the sweet, happy, outgoing young lady she had been when she left. She now had an air of darkness and brooding about her. At first I did not realize what the underlying problem was nor how severe. She was terribly thin, pale and had an unusual irritability about her. She seemed like a stranger in our home. I thought that she was exhausted and moody from finishing a tough first year but then discovered that she had become heavily involved in drugs while away at school. It started with smoking marijuana for fun which became a crutch and perhaps an excuse for her loneliness. As the depression became more pronounced, she reached to methamphetamines to "make her feel better." The combination of "pot" and "speed" along with her own low tolerance level, led to severe problems. I didn't know how to deal with this dilemma.

My daughter and I both ended up in therapy. I learned that I had inadvertently contributed to her problem of depression. As a single mom, she had always been number one in my life and when she went off to college, I felt a desire to hold on tighter in fear of losing her. The cord that one time bonded us actually became a rope in a "tug of war." I was trying to maintain the status quo while she was trying to move away from me and gain independence. I learned that my lack of trust in her abilities had undermined her self-esteem and her drug use was partly a rebellion against my holding so tightly.

Our family therapy was both a mind and life altering experience. We both made it through safely but as I look back, I realize the whole period represented by far, the most challenging time of my life.

Both of these cases were emergency situations that required professional help. As parents, we tend to fear the worst. It is important to stay in touch with our children, ask questions, be good listeners and, in a balanced way, remain open and aware of such possibilities. Most times, if trouble is suspected, getting personally involved and finding outside professional help is the best course for a positive outcome.

Steff

The times I perhaps missed my parents the most were when I wasn't feeling well physically or emotionally. I tried not to worry or bother them. I realized there was little they could do from so many miles away. I tried to take good care of myself when feeling under-the-weather but, at times, was homesick for a cup of Mom's homemade soup, or one of Dad's cheer up visits. For me, only Mom or Dad could soothe a serious ailment. The first time I felt lousy, I called Mom to ask her advice. I knew I was burning up with fever but had no one nearby to help me and nothing to eat or drink in the dorm room. Everything Mom suggested I take, I didn't have! I didn't even have a thermometer to check my temperature. As sick as I felt, the college infirmary was the last place I wanted to go. I was miserable. I finally realized the infirmary was the only place I could get help, so I went, got some medicine, and came back to my room to rest. The next morning I felt much better. I learned *that* lesson the hard way.

My roommate had a more serious bout with illness. She caught mononucleosis (everyone's worst nightmare) during the second week of school. She felt terrible and had no energy to do any of the fun freshman activities or go to class. Her problem also caused a bit of a clog in my every day life. I had to tiptoe around our room, in the dark, with blinds closed in order for her to sleep. I tried not to disturb her, but that was nearly impossible. She was really sick, and I couldn't do much to help her. The situation became difficult for both of us. She eventually went to the infirmary where she stayed for a few days. Her case proved to be a mild one, and she was soon able to return to her classes.

Mono is extremely contagious (I wasn't worried for myself since I had already had it). Within the next two weeks, two neighboring students came down with it. The advice for those who haven't had it: wash hands often and don't share food or drinks!

STRESSES ON CAMPUS

The busy life at school can cause havoc to students' physical and mental health. The environment is loaded with all kinds of stresses: challenging school assignments, noisy dorm life, outside activities, and relationship challenges. Too much stress can contribute to illness and it is important to learn how to guard against being "stressed out" even while dealing with new situations. When possible, fit in healthy activities such as exercise, walks, or finding a spot for reflection or even a nap. The emphasis during the quiet moments should be on taking time to refocus and relieve tension.

IS THE THERAPIST IN?

It was rewarding to find some friends at school supporting me when I was facing minor challenges. However, when my world seemed to really fall apart, the only person I felt safe with was Mom. The first few times I needed her shoulder, it was second nature to simply dial "home." Mom was there for me. After the phone call I felt better. Really, I think I only wanted to unload my frustrations and confusions on someone I could trust. Sometimes it was therapeutic for me to share my concerns through e-mail before I went to bed. It was like keeping a personal journal.

Sometimes temporary problems such as worry over a test, a poor grade, or an argument with a friend, seemed big to me. Initially, I tended to unload all my concerns and troubles on Mom. Eventually, I learned to sort out the more important problems and tried to deal with the lesser ones on my own.

The only drawbacks were that after I unloaded my concerns on Mom, she kept asking how the situation was even after I felt the issue had been resolved. It sometimes got on my nerves and, at times, I regretted sharing some issues with her. There were also times that I did not agree with her advice, especially when she gave it without my asking for it!

My friends, at the same time, seemed to count on me for their problems. In all of the madness of the busy academic life, I felt the pressure of being a good listener and friend-in-need. My lesson was to learn to emotionally take care of myself *first* and then help my friends.

DEPRESSION

Some situations become very serious, and it is difficult to know how best to deal with them. In my case, one of my best friends started to behave in a different and unusual manner. I was unsure how to handle it. She didn't want to join in normal activities, she stopped going to classes and she stayed in bed for days. I tried to voice my concern but it seemed to make no difference. I spoke to her roommate but could not engage her in trying to figure out what the problem was. I sensed my friend was going through some form of depression but did not know how to handle it.

I felt tremendous relief when, one day, her concerned parents called me to ask if anything was wrong. They had sensed problems since they had no contact from her and she was not answering her phone. I told them what I knew about the situation and found that she had previously had bouts with depression and perhaps was not taking her prescribed medicine. Quickly, her parents got her the necessary help. She dropped out of school that semester, went home for rest and therapy and returned much healthier in the spring.

THE LURE OF NEW EXPERIENCES

Being on our own feels great! With parents absent, what we do, how we do it, and with whom is not immediately questioned. As liberating as this can feel, this new freedom can lead to serious problems.

Let's face it, easy availability of alcohol and drugs is a reality in today's college life. Alcohol is the biggest and most popular "drug" at college. It doesn't seem to have the stigma of other drugs and students have fun telling stories with each other about their various drinking experiences. The risks, however, can still be enormously high. Students under the influence of alcohol can jeopardize themselves, their friends or even complete strangers. I must admit that there were times I put myself in high risk situations and, subsequently, was glad I made it home safely. Recognizing the critical difference between moderate social drinking and excessive drinking is important.

Besides alcohol, there are other drug experiences that can be tempting to the new college student. As a freshman, I personally was aware of incidents with drugs that I had never heard of before. A variety of substances are available through various avenues. Availability, curiosity and peer pressure can lead to actions with serious consequences for young people. Further danger is imminent when the student chooses to mix substances.

TAKING RESPONSIBILITY

Students do need to take responsibility for their own behavior. Believe it or not, "designated drivers" are more common with today's party scenes then years ago. Thankfully, most college students are taking the need for this safety practice much more seriously then in the past. Within my group of friends, when we go off campus, we share the responsibility of being the "d.d." for the night.

Without evidence to the contrary, parents should not worry unduly that substance abuse is a problem for their students. College students, in general, get stereotyped as "party animals" but I believe that this is overstating the problem. Although alcoholism and drug use does raise serious problems for some students, my friends and I are convinced that this is not a problem for the majority.

As a student, you know that substance abuse might be a serious problem when fellow students start missing classes, lose motivation, put off personal responsibilities, and begin blaming teachers and others for their falling grades. If parents sense it is a possible problem for their own child, they should get involved by talking with their child, to his or her friends, the resident advisor and/or a counselor. If there is a problem, trained professionals are the best source for help. If the child is away, look for help and programs in his or her vicinity or even bring the child home to get help.

SAFETY IN NUMBERS

There were two cases of sexual assault near campus during my freshman and sophomore years. In each case, the girls were walking home intoxicated and *alone* from parties not far from campus. Although the incidents were off-campus, the college took it seriously and arranged for the local police to speak at the dorms, sororities and fraternities on safety issues and, as a result, we learned to travel in groups. On any campus at any college, *no matter what gender*, it is safer to be accompanied by someone when walking home from a party, bar or nearby gathering. My friends and I make it a habit to look out for each other.

New found freedom can also bring about inappropriate sexual behavior. Date rape exists. Be aware of the company you keep. Share with a friend or roommate where you are going and with whom. Take responsibility for yourself.

College represents a new stage in life. The opportunities for new experiences of all kinds will be available. Awareness, common sense and prudence should all be used when faced with this new freedom of choice.

Trap Doors
Tips from Mom for parents:

· Listen first!

It is difficult not to jump in with quick judgments or advice when our children call for help. It is best, by phone, to listen carefully, ask questions about how they are feeling, try as best one can to understand the true nature of their concerns and finally, make suggestions. After that, for problems that are not too serious or life-threatening, it is best to try to "detach."

At this stage of our lives, our children are young adults, and all we can do as parents is to listen and provide our best advice. It is the responsibility of the child to either follow the advice or do otherwise. For most parents, it is finding the right balance in the "detaching" part that is difficult.

· More about depression.

Depression is the most common psychological problem among college students. Parents need to understand its causes as best they can. The stage of development during which the child is separated from the parent may be directly involved with a depressive disorder. Most new college students are away from home for the first time dealing with a variety of stressful factors: hectic schedules and possibly disappointing grades; the threat of losing a scholarship; the breaking-up of a relationship; rejection from new social groups and other stressors. These stresses can cause brief phases of depression and anxiety for college students. Most will cope and, given time, pull themselves out of these phases.

· Look for danger signs.

If there is definite evidence of problems that appear more serious, intervention by the parents might be necessary. Some more serious signs and symptoms to look for:

1. sleeping excessively
2. sleeplessness
3. missing classes
4. lack of interest in peers and social activities
5. extreme weight loss or weight gain
6. unusual moodiness
7. a marked change in hygiene habits
8. a "forced " cheerfulness

If such signs are appearing and dialogue with the student is open, parents can help by encouraging him/her to use campus resources. There are good counseling services on most campuses and the counselors know what symptoms to look for and how to treat them. Sometimes circumstances might warrant contact with the roommate or friend or possibly the floor or Resident Advisor of the dorm. This should be done with care and tact. Depending on what is learned, it could be timely and wise to share with your child your feelings and, if appropriate, discuss a plan for corrective action.

Tips from Steff for students:

· **Know the possible repercussions of "unloading" problems on your parents.**
Know that once you unload your problem on your parents, whether it involves school affairs, relationships, homesickness or just being unhappy, they will worry about it even more than you do. If you have a boyfriend or girlfriend who hurts you, it can take much longer for your parents to forgive him or her than it will for you (if they ever do forgive). Whether we like it or not, our parents take on our problems and it's sometimes hard for them to let go.
· **Advice on being under the weather:**
Sickness spreads easily in college atmospheres, a

consequence of the close living quarters and the amount of time people spend together, sharing drinks, food and space.

The best advice is:

· Don't share drinks and food

· Wash your hands often...that's where we pick up most of our germs! (I kept little bottles of disinfectant gel near my bed that I used often.)

· Get rest. I found this was not always easy in a dorm. Yes, it is noisy 24 hours a day, 7 days a week and I, too, didn't want to miss out on any action!

· Use the infirmary when feeling under the weather. I refused to do this at first but eventually concluded it was the best place I could get some sound medical help away from home.

· Talk to your family doctor about getting shots and vaccinations for such illnesses as influenza, hepatitis and meningitis. Most school infirmaries, for a small fee, offer some of these on campus.

· **If you conclude that a friend has a serious problem!**

Don't ignore it, try to do something helpful. Use your judgment in trying to communicate this to someone who can help. Depending on circumstances, this could be the resident advisor, your friend's parents, a mutual friend, or even health professionals. Do not leave the problem unattended because someone suffering from depression or serious emotional problems can make bad decisions that may change or even end his or her life. (It's frightening, but true.)

· **Advice on alcohol and drugs.**

In the end, you have to be accountable for your *own* actions. New freedom can bring the possibility of sampling new experiences. Be very selective in what these are. Do not fall victim to the abuse of drugs and alcohol. There might be opportunities for binge-drinking and competitions to "out drink" someone else. For most, the accessibility of drugs on campuses will be an eye-opener. It is likely that in college you might see some things happen that you have never seen before. Some behaviors can be shocking. Just be aware and careful. Try to make the best judgments on whether and how you participate.

When at an off-campus social event, bar or club, never let a stranger get you a beverage. Always keep an eye on your glass. Being responsible means not allowing someone to put something lethal or dangerous in your drink. A stranger's sick prank can cause havoc or possibly even death. Be aware this can happen.

For parents:

· **On alcohol and drugs:**

It is too easy for parents to take the "not my kid" approach when it comes to thinking about the potential problems of drugs and alcohol at school. Colleges are aware of the problem and do what they can to control it. No matter how strong the school policy is against it, the reality is that alcohol and drugs are available in many forms for college students. Don't be blind to the fact that experimenting does take place. For you, the parent, it is about awareness and communication.

This does not mean to assume the worse without any evidence and to be overly suspicious of your child. It requires a fine balance to do it just right. If you become convinced there is a problem, you should be ready to step in, you might be saving a very important life.

Chapter 6

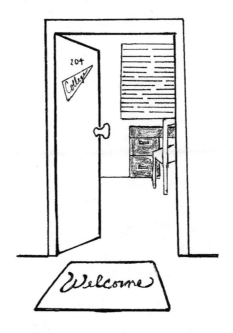

PARENTS' WEEKEND
The Open Door

Chapter 6..............

PARENTS' WEEKEND
The Open Door

The first visit for Mom and Dad on campus places the welcome mat at the *child's door*. For most, Parents' Weekend is perhaps the first time that parents get to see their young adults since they left for college. This event offers an opportunity for the parent to observe campus life in action, meet their offspring's new friends, visit with the school administration, and, importantly, get a firsthand reading on their child's adjustment to the new life. It is also the first time, perhaps, that parents feel a form of role-reversal with the child being more in control.

Mom

   I remember my excitement anticipating Parents' Weekend! I had studied all of the information from the university including the schedule of events, and it looked like a busy two days. I sensed Steffany's excitement about the visit, and this meant a lot to me. We made our reservations at a hotel fairly close to the campus.

For divorced families, the question can arise regarding which parents are going to Parents' Weekend. In some situations, this creates some tough decisions and discomfort for everyone involved. In our case, three of us were going to this event: mother; father and stepfather. Luckily, we have an amicable relationship, and Steffany seemed happy that all three of us were coming (although not arriving together). The agenda was packed with activities for the parents: meetings, lunch with the college President, a football game and concerts. My husband and I arrived, checked in and immediately headed over to the university to see my daughter.

The campus was buzzing with excitement as all ages bustled about, many sporting university-logo shirts and hats. Parents and grandparents could be seen aimlessly wandering around the student center, school store and dorms somewhat bemused as they followed the lead of their confident student-children.

It was during this weekend that we got the first inkling of role-reversal. Steffany gladly accepted our offer of lunch and led us across the crowded campus, occasionally stopping to hug various friends and making introductions. At the campus restaurant, she directed us to the food line, ordered our lunch choices, collected our tickets and found us a table. I felt as disoriented as a child lost and looking for direction in a shopping mall. The only familiar activity in this experience for us was paying the bill!

Clearly, our daughter had taken charge of the program and we were the guests. During our visit, she guided us confidently about the campus, the adjacent areas, and even the big city outside of the school community. She made the suggestions for dinner, guided us to the local spots and gave us an exciting taste of nightlife in her new hometown. I watched in amazement as she took control of the weekend. We were happy to follow her recommendations. As a parent, I felt proud and at the same time, somewhat deprived in *my* role.

I noticed that the "age of embarrassment" of having your parent around was not a factor for us. This pleased me tremendously. Arm and arm, my daughter walked me around campus. I felt that she was proud to have me by her side. I observed Steffany as I had never before. I didn't want her to feel that I was keeping an eye on her, but I felt a wonderful sense of pride as I could see a new level of independence and confidence.

On the other hand, don't be surprised if the child's response toward having parents visit is somewhat distant. The child's need might be to prove independence. Be aware. One disappointed single-mother shared her memory of visiting her son:

I didn't sense a warm welcome when Tim met me in his dorm lobby. To be outgoingly friendly was not his style. However, we hadn't seen each other in months and in my heart I was hoping for more. I was also on my own for most of the weekend as I attended the college functions. Tim didn't want to go to the football game, so I went back to my motel instead of attending it by myself. I took my son out for dinner on the first night but discovered that he had made plans with his friends for the next evening. Being alone as a visitor didn't help matters but not having Tim make himself available for the functions was disappointing. I'm not sure the decision for me to visit was the right one for either of us, but, as it is, I am sure my disappointment was deeper.

In general, students can have varying degrees of comfort about their parents' campus visit. So much depends on existing family relationships, and these should be considered carefully when decisions on the visit are being made. If the student really wants it, and if timing and finances permit, the parent(s) should make a strong effort to be there. At best, it can be a great opportunity to build on a relationship. The parents can show pride, trust and friendship; and the student independence, leadership and, hopefully, pride. At the end of the day, most students will enjoy being taken off campus by their parents for a good restaurant meal.

Parents' Weekend is an opportunity to meet the student's new friends and their parents. In our case, we joined with other families to attend some of the events such as the football game, on-campus activities and meals. It was nice to exchange observations and experiences with other parents. And to our daughter's friends whose parents could not be present for the weekend, we opened the invitation to join us for meals. We hoped they enjoyed it; we know we did.

I felt I was adjusting very well to school and was enjoying the surroundings, classes and friends. I truly looked forward to my parents coming down for Parents' Weekend. It was amusing to us, as students, to see how the school, itself, was concentrating on doing things to impress the visiting parents: the school grounds were being manicured, paths raked, grass cut, new shrubbery and flowers added along some of the buildings. We wondered what all the fuss was about until the older students filled us in on the ritual of buildup for the upcoming arrival of parents. After all, colleges and universities live in a competitive world, too.

From the moment I heard the knock at my dorm door, I felt the weekend was going to be a blast. My parents were on *my* turf and it was my responsibility to show them a good time. I was excited to take them to meet my friends.

Mom and I did a few things on our own and had a nice chance to talk. She met me for lunch, a walk, and a workout at the college wellness center. It was nice to have her by my side. We talked like girlfriends as she seemed so interested in my new life. Otherwise, my dad, step-dad, mom and I attended the planned festivities and made the most of the weekend. The best part was eating meals off campus!

Let's talk *eating* out. I accentuate the word "eat" because freshman girls can eat! I watched my parents' eyes bulging as they saw four girls shovel appetizers, main meals, and desserts into their mouths. My friends and I were thrilled with the flavor of restaurant food. The on-campus food, although not bad, was high in starch and carbohydrates and less exciting. We were ready for a change in menus. With our budgets limited at school, we could not afford fancy restaurants. Our steady diet was a lot of pizza, pasta and soft-serve ice cream. Believe me, college kids learn the value of the dollar really quickly when it is *their* money they are spending. It is special to be taken out to eat!

As much as I looked forward to having my parents visit, I must admit that I was unsure as to how the weekend might go. I happily found my parents relaxed and not trying to monopolize my time. They seemed comfortable with what I wanted to do and with whom I wanted to have join us. Introducing my friends to them went smoothly and I was proud to introduce them to each other. There seemed to be no judgments made and no competition for control of the weekend. I was in charge as they let me plan the days and evenings with no hassles. After a stressed-out summer with so many responsibilities being shoved down my throat, this was a pleasant surprise.

The only conflict of the weekend arose after we had finished dinner on Saturday night. I couldn't help but notice how seemingly early my family wanted to retire back to their hotels. It was only just after eleven p.m. and my friends and I were ready to continue the evening. My dad commented that he felt it was time to go back to the dorm. To me and my friends, it was early! I was on my turf and had no rules. After Dad dropped us off at the dorm, we went to an off-campus party. The next day, there was a raised eyebrow but no major fuss when Dad found out.

Trap Doors

Tips from Mom for parents:

- **During the visit, let your child assume some responsibility and take a leadership role.**

This is the first experience during which I personally felt *role-reversal*. The responsibility was on my daughter's shoulders as she planned the visit, showed us around the area, introduced us to friends and colleagues, and truly took charge. Suddenly, I was aware of her blossoming maturity. Although it was a new experience for me, it was a positive one. There were moments, however, when I felt a mother's need to control, but I chose, instead, to try to relax and let her be the responsible one. It wasn't always easy but I actually enjoyed it.

- **Book early for hotel reservations.**

Parents' Weekends are well-attended. Book early in order to get accommodations that are conveniently located.

- **When possible, extend invitations to your children's college friends.**

Everything is geared for the family on this weekend. For those young adults who are alone, it is nice to feel included in family activities. They, too, enjoy being taken off-campus for activities or a shared meal.

Tips from Steff for students:

· **Plan some personal time with your parents.**

Parents' Weekend is full of activities that can be somewhat fast-paced and overwhelming for all, so make sure to schedule some time alone with your parents, *without* your friends.

· **Make things "presentable."**

Clean up your clothes, try to straighten up your room and make things as presentable as possible. It is amazing how impressed or shocked parents can be to see organization and neatness!

· **Before your parents' plans are etched in concrete, share your feeling about their attendance.**

If you do not want to take part in Parents' Weekend and feel extremely uncomfortable about having your parents visit, be open with them.

For parents:

· Try to be open-minded about what your child wants to do, and don't be surprised if your student wants to have both your company and the company of friends.

· If you go out to dinner, don't be offended if your student wants to go out with his/her friends afterwards even though you feel they should be ready for bed; remember, you're on their turf.

· Offer to take your student off-campus for shopping or meals. For him or her, to have the opportunity to see the outside world is a real treat.

Chapter 7

FIRST VISIT HOME
The Door Jam

Chapter 7..............

FIRST VISIT HOME
The Door Jam

In most family situations, the first homecoming will be anticipated with some degree of excitement. The student's return to the nest will bring back some familiar feelings to all members. For the family at home, the house feels as it used to be. Hopefully, for the returning student, the accustomed surrounds, comfortable bed, and home-cooked meals will make the visit a welcoming oasis.

The reality is that along with warm feelings, the visit can bring some challenges. "Home sweet home" can take on new and different definitions for parents and child when the latter settles in for this particular visit. Parents expect their child to return to the old set of house-rules while the young-adult expects to continue his new found sense of independence. The *door jam* represents some of the awkward and sometimes difficult circumstances and misunderstandings that can get in the way of a peaceful homecoming. With awareness and open communication from all parties, the return can be a more positive experience.

Mom

THE HOUSE IS ALIVE AGAIN!

I counted the days until Steffany's school break. Suddenly, it was here:

December 18 (Journal entry)

As I go to bed tonight, my excitement soars! Steffany is coming home tomorrow morning. I have shopped for her favorite foods and am planning on baking and fixing her favorite dishes. Home will seem more complete again.

The house was awaiting Steffany's arrival. Her room was ready, the fridge was full, and menus were planned to include her favorite dishes. I couldn't seem to get to the airport fast enough! As busy as the airport was for the holiday, I decided to meet her at the gate. I smiled to myself when I saw numerous parents just like me, anxiously awaiting their home-bound college children. Anticipation had my heart pounding with excitement. How would she look? Is she more mature? Is she happy to be coming home? Finally, as I waited by the airport ramp, I saw a mature-looking and confident young woman walking toward me. Our ride home was filled with positive energy as she shared news about college and her friends.

As soon as we got home, the house came alive. An hour didn't go by without the phone ringing. Shortly thereafter, the doorbell was ringing, the stereo was playing, and before the night was over, cars were parked in our driveway; and laughter, yelps, and enthusiastic, nonstop conversation echoed throughout our house. My husband and I observed the way the activity broke the peaceful environment to which we had grown accustomed for the last few months. At that moment, I didn't mind at all. As a matter of fact, I loved it.

I sent the following to Penny, my good friend and mother of a college freshman:

> **From**: mom@aol.com
> **To**: mom2@aol.com
> **Date**: Dec. 19

> *Hopefully, this e-mail finds you enjoying your entire family at home as much as I am enjoying mine. The sound of voices, the snacking on munchies and leftovers in the kitchen, the phone ringing, the stereo and MTV playing...it is great! Who ever thought I'd say this?*

THE TENSION BEGINS...

Within the first 48 hours, the situation began to lose its early excitement as I realized differences in schedules, attitudes and behaviors. Days for my husband and me typically ended at 11:00 p.m. We normally rose reasonably early for our daily routines. Even in our conservative community, our college freshman's evenings *began* at 11:00 p.m., and her need to regain energy meant sleeping until at least noon the next day! We concluded we couldn't support her timetable, and she couldn't understand ours.

Soon, I found myself debating with Steffany on her new schedule: the hour she was going out, the time she was coming in, and the ridiculous hour she woke up. I was insistent that her curfew remain at 1:00 a.m. which it had been during her high school senior year. "One a.m.? Are you kidding?" She would say, "Mom, I'm now an adult on my own. Please recognize I have no curfew at school!"

Despite each of our headstrong stances, we negotiated to extend the curfew to 2:00 a.m. Unfortunately, neither of us was happy with this agreement. I felt I had given at least as much as I could, but my daughter felt it wasn't enough. My challenge was being able to fall asleep before she came home. For those parents who can't fall off into deep slumber until they hear the door open and the keys hit the counter, extended night sleeps are gone. Matters were made worse by the fact that the late night schedule included week nights. To college students home from school and *not* working a job, every night seemed to be treated as a weekend night.

One frustrated parent, whose freshman son was home for his break, commented:

I was exhausted! I was waiting up for my son and not getting a decent night's sleep. I explained to Dan that I needed him to come home on weeknights by midnight in order for me to have the energy to get up at 6:00 a.m. for work. He responded sarcastically, "Let's get this straight, so what you're telling me is that I have to come in early so you can go to work? Something is wrong here!"

My frustration continued as I noticed our daughter's formerly clean and tidy bedroom take on a new look—explosive! Clothes were strewn everywhere outside of closets and drawers, suitcases unemptied in the corners, bath towels and CD's on the floor, and papers and unrecognizable odds and ends adorning every flat surface. What had college dorm life done to Steffany's housekeeping habits?

Tension at home began to increase. My enthusiasm about the household regaining its "full nest" status was waning. As I watched my bedroom digital clock turning to 2:15 a.m. (waiting for her arrival home), as I stepped over the mess in her bedroom to *find* her ringing phone to answer it, as I picked up dirty dishes and trails of empty soda cans throughout the house (from the college social set), and as I found myself whispering and tiptoeing in my *own* household at 12 noon while my daughter still slept, my frustration started to turn into anger. There were even moments that I consoled myself by counting the days until she again would be back at school.

I did not like what I was feeling. I was confused and disappointed. I felt that I hardly knew this person who had come home from school. Our relationship seemed to have changed. Where was life as it used to be here at home?

Despite it all, lessons were being learned. . .

COMING HOME!

With school break approaching, there was definitely something in the air on campus. I believe that "something" was intense excitement toward everyone's first extended visit home. In my case, this meant both the pool and the gym were packed 24-7. As females in a southern school, most of my friends wanted to go home with tans and in-shape tushes. I laugh about it, but I won't lie and tell you I wasn't doing the same thing. This, however, was not so easy considering the extra pounds that college life had added to our behinds. I was exhausted due to late nights and the stress of final exams. Even though I had little energy at this point, I had not realized how much was involved in prepping to go home!

I had heard how things change when you return home such as people, places, the former high school and home itself. I was anxious to see my parents, eat home-cooked food, and enjoy the comfort and safety of home, but not without a little nervous hesitation about how things would go.

SEEING OLD FRIENDS

I was immensely excited by the prospect of seeing my old friends from home. I had kept in touch with many on a regular basis and was eager to see how they looked and to share our experiences as freshmen.

I had a ball when I first returned home. A bunch of my friends had gathered at the house, and we sat and gabbed all night about school, weather, sports, friends and, of course, cute guys and girls. Everyone was so excited to tell their stories about "When I went out...." or "You'll never guess who I met...." Looking back on it now, it seems funny, because we were all trying to outdo each other's stories. For the moment, it was fun and I felt good about myself.

I was uncomfortable, though, as I heard my old friends talk about their new "best friends" at college. In a way, I felt a little jealous and betrayed, even though this was somewhat hypocritical of me since I had my new "best" friends as well. It felt awkward. Here I was, back with the people with whom I grew up, and something was missing. I felt that we had missed a big part of each others' lives over the past four months.

TENSION ON THE HOMEFRONT

As I look back, I probably should have handled my Christmas break differently than I did. At Thanksgiving, the break was only for a few days, but I utilized those days to the fullest extent. There was so much I wanted to do and people that I wanted to see that I made no real quality time for my parents. But, for this short visit, everybody seemed happy enough with events. I felt that Christmas break would allow me more time to visit with my family, but, looking back, I can recognize that my primary focus was on trying to catch up with my old friends.

My absorption in my social life seemed to upset my parents. Both my mom and my dad indicated they would appreciate more time with me. I felt that being home was enough. Mom wanted to do things with me, even run errands with her in the car so we could visit. I certainly did not enjoy running to the cleaners, grocery store and gas station with her . . . I *never* enjoyed that. Dad, too, expected time with me but, as it can be after a divorce, time with him was usually spent at a restaurant or at a movie. This was okay because I would go out with my friends afterwards.

During the extended break, Mom and I seemed to argue about everything: my sleeping late, the condition of my bedroom, dirty dishes in the kitchen sink, not eating meals with the family, poor eating habits and, perhaps above all, my late hours. From my perspective, I couldn't imagine what had gone wrong with Mom. She seemed to expect my schedule to remain as it was when I was in high school.

My parents did not seem to understand that weekends *and* weeknights were for socializing. This, after all, was my vacation. Too many questions were fired at me: "Where are you going?" "What time are you going to be home?" "Who else is going?" "Who's driving?" "Are they responsible?" I would reply to all of these questions with the most common answer among college students, "I don't know!"

These questions irked me considering I had survived well at college for a few months on my *own* schedule, making my *own* plans and not having to answer to anybody else. I had anticipated that the social life and schedule I had at school would come home with me with the added blessings of no studies, no reasons to get up early, plenty of home-cooked meals, and the availability of my hometown batch of friends.

To put it mildly, I soon sensed that this wasn't exactly what my parents had in mind. I'll admit that I had neglected some of their interests, but I had been extremely upset when they asked me so many questions and expected me to follow the old house-rules. In my college environment, I was used to being treated as an adult while living independently, and I didn't know how to act as a dependent again. Despite the comforts of home, I started to look forward to being back at school with my own schedule and life.

For the first time in my life, I felt that my mom did not trust me. This was confusing and hurtful to me since she had always seemed to have trusted me in the past. After several serious arguments and shouting matches, we called a truce and dedicated time to discuss our differences and how what was going on made each of us feel. This was an important step. I guess we both had some lessons to learn: as the child (guest) in the house, I had to learn to respect the household (my family); Mom, on the other hand, needed to relax more, "let go" and trust me.

We've learned over these years that similar issues continue to pop-up during each extended visit home. To deal with this, Mom and I have consciously decided to share what is on our minds early and not let the tension build up because of unspoken concerns. Our private talks take place on long walks together, or we go to a favorite place for lunch. We have learned a lot about how to share our sometime different viewpoints in a more constructive manner.

Trap Doors:
Tips from Mom for parents:

· **Be prepared for your child's independent attitude.**
It's true, our children have been living lives on their own schedules at school. Plan to discuss the desired household rules and guidelines with respect to curfews, schedules and housekeeping early in the first visit home. Be prepared to negotiate. . . any person capable of attending college will expect that and deserves it.
· **Find and make time to spend with your child.**
When possible, try to set aside time to spend as family time. Whether it be doing an activity or sport or having a meal together, this segment of time gives you opportunity, as a family, to share. Make sure that it is something that each enjoys doing.

Tips from Steff for students:

- **Understand that rules haven't necessarily changed at home.**

Don't be surprised to find that your parents expect you to follow the old house-rules when you return home. Be prepared to discuss what they expect, suggest what changes might help you and be as open-minded as possible.

- **Be prepared for some awkwardness with your old friends from home.**

At first, visiting with your hometown friends might seem strange. Each of you have been experiencing a major life transition with distance between you. If you are good friends, this awkwardness won't last and will not change your friendship; it just puts it in a different light.

Chapter 8

THE RETURN TO COLLEGE
Doors Apart II

Chapter 8...............

THE RETURN TO COLLEGE
Doors Apart II

The first extended visit home for the student brought new learnings for both generations. When the child returns to college, the second separation can create new kinds of feelings. For parents, it is back to a more quiet, neater and worry-free household with possibly some emptiness that was felt during the first semester's departure.

For the student, it is back to class schedules, dining hall meals, campus social activities, and more personal freedom. After revisiting the comforts of home, the readjustment for the student can sometimes be more difficult than expected.

Mom
ON THE PARENT-CHILD RELATIONSHIP
There were both joys and challenges during Steffany's

Christmas break. Her return home brought the still familiar atmosphere of *life before college:* a noisy and active household, more laundry to do and errands to run, meals with the entire family around the table and the sharing of a family car. But it didn't take long to discover that transitions were taking place with our individual attitudes, priorities and in our relationship. Since Steffany had left for college, a tug of war had developed between us over issues surrounding her independence. At the worst times during this period, I felt like an interloper in our own household.

Somewhat to my surprise, Steffany's return to college brought back some of the feelings of emptiness that I had experienced when she first left home. These feelings coincided with a growing appreciation for my own freedom. Steffany was back at college, and her room looked bare with a scattering of remnants from her visit. The incoming phone calls were minimal. In truth, I missed Steffany's presence in the house and unavoidably, my household responsibilities as "Mom" were put on hold until the next homecoming.

At the same time, there was a sense of relief that we could have a moratorium in the bickering over house-rules and independence issues. I welcomed thoughts of good night sleeps as I realized that I would not be waiting up for Steffany's late-night socializing to end. Not being so close to her social schedule and activities helped me to relax. Out of sight, fewer worries. There was no question that the visit had brought new challenges to our relationship. At this point, separation gave us a chance to digest and learn from what we had experienced. For my part, I drew comfort from the unspoken truce between Steffany and me at the airport as we hugged good-bye, knowing we were at peace despite our recent conflicts. Best of all, our love was strong.

ON RELATIONSHIPS

After a month at home, I was ready to return to school. My mother had gotten on my nerves by trying to impose what I considered were outdated house-rules. Although I didn't see as much of my dad, I noticed that he, too, expected me to be flexible in meeting *his* schedule of events. He didn't seem to notice that some of my priorities had changed. So, returning to school meant regaining much more personal freedom.

Saying good-bye to Mom was very emotional for me. So much had gone on between us over the break. I hated the conflict. I wanted to go back to my independent life at school but I wanted her to understand I still loved her.

I had talked on the phone to a few friends from college over the break but while at home, my focus was mostly on my hometown, longtime relationships. During this period, I seemed to have slipped effortlessly into my life-before-college role. Separating from my old friends was more saddening than I thought it would be. There was also a painful breakup with my high school boyfriend the day before I returned to college. We both realized that we had changed and that the distance between us was too great to let a steady commitment work. So, with all these factors, I returned to school in an emotional state.

SECOND SEMESTER BLUES

Although I was not as fearful as I was when leaving home for my first semester, I found myself more homesick in the beginning of my second. My arrival on campus was less event-filled than it was during my freshman orientation. With my spring schedule, I was excited to see new faces and meet the people in my classes. This time, I had returned to school early (perhaps too early). It was a gray and rainy day, and my roommate had not yet returned. The dorm hall was silent. I sat alone on my bed, staring at the cold, concrete walls of my room while a thousand thoughts were rushing through my head. Oh, how badly I wanted to crawl into my own bed at home and snuggle with our cat. I now felt alone. It was a peculiar feeling and one that I hadn't felt before. Images flashed before me: Mom's teary hug at the airport, my breakup with my boyfriend, my good-byes to my girlfriends, and not least, my safe and comfortable home. I cried. For the moment, being back at school was not my choice.

BACK TO NORMAL

One thing about being young, moods come and go. Once my roommate and other residents returned, I started to feel better. Life in the dorm was noisy and chaotic again and, for me, college life seemed back to where it left off. The homesickness wore off. I began to feel a new comfort and confidence as a second-semester freshman. This time, I knew my way around campus and had established friendships to revisit. The missing of my family, old friends and comforts of home quickly faded. My focus was on new classes, activities and spring. I felt a new energy toward life.

Trap Doors
Tips from Mom for parents:

· **Mixed emotions for parents.**

Expect to feel a combination of relief and sadness as your child returns to campus. Some parents may feel elated. Others may feel sad. Your household will become more quiet again and life will seem strange for the moment but just as life picks up for the student going back, it also picks up for the parent left behind. Some of these feelings can return each time your child departs for school after an extended break. This is normal. The first year, however, is the most noticeable.

· **There might be more challenges for your student on the return.**

Don't be surprised if your child conveys some signs of homesickness after this first, long visit home. Because the second semester of the freshman year is more low-key than the first, there is more opportunity to miss the comforts of home.

Tips from Steff for students:

· **Going back to school.**

Anticipate that if you go back early, the campus might seem vacant and inhospitable. If the school is empty, there will be little to do and, in some cases, the dining halls may not yet be open.

Don't be surprised if you feel a mixed bag of emotions about your return. You might feel thrilled to have your freedom back but, at the same time, miss the safety and comforts of home much more than you expected.

· **Get rest before going back.**

Try to be rested for the second semester. Once the normal schedule starts, there is little time to catch up on sleep. For health reasons, adequate rest will be important in guarding against the colds and flu that seem to appear on campus during the winter months.

Chapter 9

LIFE BEYOND THE FIRST YEAR
Door to the Future

Chapter 9...............

LIFE BEYOND THE FIRST YEAR
Door to the Future

The college years pass by more quickly than one can imagine. Like caterpillars, the youths who left the safe cocoon of home, develop their own kind of wings which they spread as they prepare to venture out into the world. Their parents observe the process in amazement as the transformation takes place. Both generations notice the seemingly rapid passage of time and begin to once again seriously ponder, "What's next?"

It can be a fulfilling experience for parents to watch their children mature. With each visit, they can not help but notice their young adult's transformation physically, emotionally and socially: the girls and boys begin to look like young men and women; conversation between parent and child becomes broader in scope and more interesting; and the personal challenges for the offspring are met with a growing sense of responsibility, independence, and maturity.

Mom

My first awareness of role-reversal was at the university
when I was a *guest* in my daughter's world. As new and
somewhat awkward as the change was for me, I worked at
trying to let her lead her own life. As time passed with each
semester, I was more aware of the shift in our relationship.
Visits home revealed her growing maturity and self
confidence, and I took pride in the change. In reality, I was
growing, too.

A New Relationship with My Daughter

Passing time changes a mother and daughter,
but not the bond they share.

There is a point during the college years when parents
discover a new relationship developing with their offspring.
As children move into adulthood and start to see and
experience new aspects of life, both generations find that
they have more in common. There is suddenly a new respect
and understanding of each other. Parents learn to listen to
advice from their children, and children learn from and
respect the wisdom of their parents.

I remember a particular experience where this insight
became very clear to me. During Steffany's second year of
college, I was invited to join her in New York at a career
conference. I was delighted and looked forward to a mother-
daughter night together. I accepted and planned to join her
for one night. She paid for the hotel on her own and I, in
turn, offered to treat her to dinner.

That evening, Steffany asked me to join her at the
orientation party. I was rather surprised but certainly
complimented that my twenty-year-old wanted the company
of her mother to such an event. I felt Steffany wanted my
support. At the same time, she wanted to demonstrate her
own initiative and independence. She asked me *not* to tell
the attendees that I was her mother; instead, she suggested

I *pretend* to be a graduate student or teacher. I smiled, thinking about her growing self reliance. So, for the occasion, I joined her incognito.

At the event, I did not want to lie about my identity, so I played a wall flower, avoided conversation, and stood back to watch the activity. This had its own rewards. I was touched as I watched my daughter confidently move about the room, introducing herself, taking control of the moment but occasionally checking back with me to see if *I* was all right. Perhaps there was also a touch on her part of, "Am I doing okay?"

Roles shifted again later when I took Steffany to dinner. I was the one in *my* comfort zone as I took her under my wing to a favorite restaurant of mine. The evening brought a potpourri of emotions for both of us as we laughed, cried, asked questions, and shared stories and bits of wisdom. We behaved like good friends catching up on each other's lives. I remember her eyes lighting up when I described my experiences at an age not much different from her own. After dinner, we returned to the hotel and stayed up until the wee hours chatting like girlfriends at a teenage sleep-over.

The next day, I left with a sense of comfort realizing that a more adult relationship between my daughter and me was developing. I felt more confidence in her decisions and actions. I was beginning to see my child's transformation and was pleased at what I was seeing.

THE FIRST APARTMENT

Steffany's junior year brought her the challenge and excitement of moving out of the dorm. I worried about her living off-campus and out of the safety-net of the university. She and her roommate shopped with a real estate broker, found a place to call "home" and then searched for a third roommate to make it affordable. This was another step in their maturing process.

Steffany's father co-signed for legal reasons and my

responsibility was to help her furnish the new home on a limited budget. Both her roommate's mother and I visited and found mixed pleasures playing cleaners, decorators and advisors. Our biggest concern was safety, and we felt relieved that the apartment was equipped with double locks and an alarm system. For us, the visit was physically exhausting but great fun.

There can be challenges in living off-campus that do not exist on campus. Good landlords can be hard to find. More common are co-tenants who don't obey house-rules, don't pay their share of bills on a timely basis, and have "different from expected" living habits. Additionally, expenses will always be more than budgeted. If the mix of tenants is a good one, each will realize their responsibilities and fulfill them. Living off-campus can be a fun and a learning experience.

As the pre-designated manager of the apartment, Steffany had her own challenges. The toughest was asking one of the apartment mates to move out. He was not abiding by some of the agreed-upon rules and had brought in a significant other to live rent free. Steffany, as the co-signer of the lease, but also a good friend of the co-tenant, had to face up to the responsibility of asking him to leave. She did just that, and it all worked out better than she had imagined. For Steffany, it was another step in learning how to make decisions and take responsibility. . .welcome to life.

Another mother shared details of a disastrous housing arrangement that her daughter had entered into:

Carol wanted to move into an apartment during her junior year. She told me that she wanted to be more independent and had found a cute house off-campus. I went to visit and was mortified. It was in what I considered an unsafe part of town, too small for three roommates and needed a lot of attention. Despite my concerned and adverse comments, my daughter was determined to move in. I finally decided to keep quiet. Her first week was spent with no water supply which meant no toilet facilities of any kind.

Her roommates, whom she thought she knew, turned out to be heavy smokers and had constant visitors coming and going. Despite her complaints, nothing changed. Carol became miserable and eventually "third person out" in the apartment. Unfortunately, because of her scholarship requirements, she had to stay put through the rest of the school year. The situation became a nightmare but one she had to endure.

LESSONS IN LIFE AFTER COLLEGE

For some students close to graduation, the approaching responsibility of being on their own in the world outside of college can be frightening. A recent study by Arthur Levine of Columbia University indicates that a significant percentage of students are concerned about being able to cope with today's world. To a large extent, their fears are caused by increasing pressures in society and expectations and judgments from parents and peers. Additionally, the fast-moving, technology-driven world is, in many ways, more challenging than it used to be.

Today, many students return home after graduation unsure of what they want to do. Parents want to feel that their offspring are ready to be on their own. They want to know that their young ones have a good sense of what the world is about and ambition to succeed in it.

Consequently, life out there can be intimidating. So, while encouraging their move towards independence, as parents, we should pay continuing and careful attention to what is going on inside the minds of our young adults. For some time, they may need a sounding board for their evolving thoughts and feelings.

A New Relationship with My Mom

As college years advanced, I began to notice a different relationship developing with my mom. Our relationship seemed to grow even closer. When I say "closer," I mean that we better understood each other. I hadn't realized how much I had matured during my college years, but I know she had. She would compliment me for taking increasing responsibility for matters in my life. That made me feel good. Our communication became more open and direct. The change wasn't as an epiphany; it was something that happened that I appreciated over time.

Our understanding and tolerance for each others' idiosyncrasies in communication grew. Freshman year could be described as a "push-pull" year for us. At one moment, I was pushing my mom away and at another, I was pulling her close again. I felt she was doing the same. I believe that this was subconscious and yet normal on our parts.

Mom, too, seemed to be changing. She seemed to put more trust in my decisions and was more relaxed about her involvement in my life. She still worried about me and still does! I don't like this trait in her. I can hear her saying over and over again, "You'll understand when *you* are a mother!" Well, I am not a mother and I do not fully understand this maternal feeling. I do know that despite our differences, I have grown to respect Mom even more and I work hard to try to validate the feelings she wants to express to me.

The First Apartment

Getting my own apartment in my junior year was such a great feeling. The sense of independence that I felt away at college took on a different aspect. After living with a group of males and females in a dorm environment, a private bath and bedroom was heaven! The initial steps of finding the roommates and shopping for the right place was a hassle but fun. My closest friend and I found an apartment for a larger rent than we had planned to pay but felt we could make it work. Our moms chipped in and helped decorate our new home. It was definitely a step we were excited about.

With the excitement came a variety of challenges: in relationships among the apartment mates; coping with getting landlord attention to minor problems that developed and bills, bills, bills! We began a different code of responsibilities. Living in the dorm, I was not diligent about turning off the TV or lights when I left my room. The electricity charge was included with tuition. Living off campus, I sooner learned to practice resource conservation. Food shopping seemed to cost a fortune. Transportation costs increased since I had to pay for an off-campus parking pass and used more gas driving to classes everyday.

Despite our enthusiastic start, there were relationship challenges with apartment mates. Disagreements on responsibilities were common. I spoke up on the kitchen mess since I seemed to be cleaning most of the time. Apartments can be a pleasant change from the relatively crowded conditions of the dorm but there are new responsibilities to be accepted.

CHANGING FOCUS ON STUDIES

Many high school seniors don't have a clear idea of what they want to study in college. To those who have a career path mapped out and a passion to follow through, congratulations. This is rare. Statistics show that a large number of students change their majors over the four years of college. Personally, I changed my second major (as a double major) during my junior year and found that there were additional credits I would have to make up in order to graduate. Fortunately, my parents supported my changing interests.

According to my college friends, parents aren't always

so understanding about changes in interests. One male friend of mine who was burned out and confused over career choices due to three tough years of studies, wanted to take a semester off to work and collect his thoughts toward future ambitions. His parents were closed-minded about what they seemed to regard as needless procrastination. The unfortunate conclusions to this family discussion was that he was asked to leave the home. This led to depression for this particular young man and other challenges resulted. He dropped out of college altogether.

Uncertainty over career choices is not uncommon during junior and senior years. Many college students have changed their majors up to three times in order to find what they wanted to do long-term. Despite the complications of changing majors, it is a mistake to be stuck in courses that do not fit career interests. Sadly, there is a tendency for students to bail out and go through the motions just to get through school.

LIFE AFTER COLLEGE

The main focus for the college freshman is *on school* and the main focus for the college senior is on *life after school*. Increasingly, seniors are pondering a mixture of important questions: Did I really make the right choice on what I want to do? Can I find a decent job? Will I succeed at my job? Can I make enough money to support myself in the lifestyle I desire? Will I be happy with what I choose?

The roles and attitudes of women have particularly changed over the years. While until recent times, the pressures of being able to support a family used to be on the male, now females are being faced with accepting similar responsibilities. More and more, women are having to find the right balance between work and family.

The real world approaches quickly in the last year of college and the senior can either embrace the prospect or try to hide from it. Eventually, the real world will find us all.

Trap Doors
Tips from Mom for parents:

· **Enjoy and trust.**

Step back and enjoy the growth in maturity of your child. Unless she obviously makes repeated mistakes, learn to trust her decisions.

· **Changes in interests.**

Understand that there might be logical changes in your child's interest in majors. Listen to her thoughts carefully and help steer her through the process. Be patient and as open-minded as possible.

· **Take part in the first off-campus home.**

Take part in your offspring's first apartment or home off-campus. Perhaps more than in the managed atmosphere of the campus, she needs your support and sometimes involved help.

Tips from Steff for students:

· **On apartment mates.**

If early relationships are not working well in apartment arrangements, someone should step up to communicate this and encourage discussion of what needs to change. Whether everyone starts out as friends or strangers, this can be tough. It does need to be done, however.

· **Choosing careers.**

It is important to try to choose a field about which you feel passionate. Recognize that your feelings may change during your years at college. Earning power is important, but disliking what you are doing day after day can make life miserable. Try to find the right balance.

For parents:
· **On field of study.**

With the right approach, you can be a great influence on your child in selecting what field of study is chosen. It is helpful to suggest possibilities based on your special insight into their interests as well as capabilities, but recognize that in the end, the choice should be the student's. Following in a parent's footsteps might be the wrong direction for them to go. Help them, but let them make the choice.

People of college age today have a much broader view of the world than their parents did at the same age. During the college years, understand that your child's interests and sense of priorities are changing. Try always to be open to listening, discussing, and offering opinions when asked (or if you judge the time is right).

Chapter 10

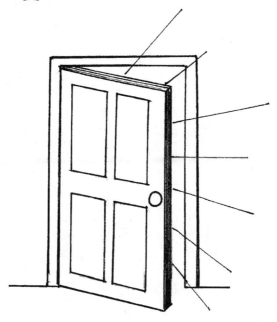

THE FINAL PHASE
Reaching the Golden Door

Chapter 10..............

THE FINAL PHASE
Reaching the Golden Door

R*eaching the golden door* represents a successful end to a journey for both generations—graduation! The journey will have been more of a challenge for some families than for others since familial circumstances can vary widely. Some family units are not together. Some young adults are completely uncertain about what they are trying to accomplish while at college. Some of these will think they know what they want but might not be motivated to try hard. Some will breeze through college and into a job. No matter what the circumstances, open communication and mutual support on the part of *both* generations can help make this final phase of the off-to-college transition a successful one.

Mom

Now the question I ask myself is, "Where did the college years go?" Four years later, the term *empty nest* has even more meaning. In our family, the transition has been made. No more am I questioning my identity or purpose in the role of mother. Nothing has been lost; new doors have opened in my day-to-day life, and a stronger mother/daughter relationship has been gained. We all have survived the transition and now look forward to the next phase.

A SPECIAL BOND

Several factors helped Steffany and me through the challenges of this transition. We fulfilled a pledge to each other to maintain open and honest communication. We now know that this was a key factor in maintaining a healthy relationship and understanding each other's needs. By sharing our thoughts and feelings, we have been able to deal with challenges as they have come one by one. Was it always smooth and easy? No. But we found ways to support one another verbally and non-verbally—with a word, a smile, a hug, or a written reminder. My most difficult challenges were suspending judgments and learning to let go. My determination to trust my daughter played an important role in this effort.

Having faith and maintaining a positive outlook were other factors that helped make this a successful transition. During our conflicts and disagreements, we made conscious choices not to dwell on past problems or on our fears. Instead, we chose to focus on the particular issue at hand.

Steff

My college experience is still difficult to capture in a few words. "The best years of your life," people say. Well, I must admit they have been the best so far, although I do not want to down play the potential of the rest of my life. I learned a lot about myself and about life in general. I learned to accept change. It is easy to fear change, but I am learning that change is a most important and inevitable element in personal growth.

At times, I felt somewhat smothered by Mom with her advice and attention to what was going on in my life. I am glad that I learned to communicate openly when I felt she was tending to treat me like a young child. With time, I learned to communicate with less anger and frustration. She seemed to develop more trust in me as I took more responsibility. In hindsight, I better understand and have appreciation for her involvement which I always knew was based on genuine love.

Each phase of my transition had its own joys and challenges. Open communication, trying to maintain a positive outlook, and a good sense of humor helped me to get through. Leaving the nest was not as easy as I initially wanted to believe it would be. I learned, however, that it is what you make of it. And *that* learning has led to my belief that future life will be what I make of it.

A Special Bond

I can compare my relationship with my mother over these past few years to a game of yo-yo—I have needed her, not needed her; liked her, disliked her; trusted her and questioned her. Although these fluctuations in my moods and attitudes have been stressful for our relationship, they prompted discussion between us and we have steadily built a better understanding of each other. I find it interesting, the older I get, the more I see characteristics of my mother in myself. Sometimes, I laugh about it; at other times, I curse it!

As I look back, despite our differences, I have always felt my mother's love and support. Our challenges in communication were important for the growth of our relationship during my college years. Life being what it is,

I know we will continue to face challenges. I also know our relationship will continue to grow.

From Both of Us

This book acknowledges some of the challenges that can exist for parents and children involving the off-to-college transition. Nurturing of the parent/child relationship, which all would accept as important in a child's early years, is still important as the child enters adulthood. We, as mother and daughter, have shared how we dealt with our own set of challenges. Writing this book encouraged us to look at our relationship without being judgmental. As we go forward to face other life transitions and challenges, we will strive to remain open minded and to learn from each other.

In our society, college is a major step in our educational process. All taking that step deserve the best chance to make this a successful transition. Hopefully, for both parent and child, as they close an important door behind them, they clearly and confidently see the next one that has opened ahead.

Notes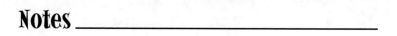

Notes

Notes

Notes

Notes

Notes

Notes

Notes

Notes